Anonymous

New Pocket Guide Throught Boston and Vicinity

Anonymous

New Pocket Guide Throught Boston and Vicinity

ISBN/EAN: 9783744760478

Printed in Europe, USA, Canada, Australia, Japan

Cover: Foto ©Andreas Hilbeck / pixelio.de

More available books at **www.hansebooks.com**

New Pocket Guide

THROUGH

Boston and Vicinity.

A Complete Handbook,

DIRECTING VISITORS

Where, When, & How to Go

THROUGH THE CITY AND SUBURBS.

WITH NEW MAP OF BOSTON.

BOSTON:
JS R. OSGOOD AND COMPANY,
(Late TICKNOR & FIELDS, and FIELDS, OSGOOD, & CO.)
131 FRANKLIN STREET.
1875.

PUBLISHERS' NOTE.

This Guide is based on "The Strangers' Guide," which has been published for several years; but it has been entirely rewritten, and brought down to date, so as to include everything of general interest to the residents of Boston, and to strangers visiting the city on account of the Centennial Celebrations and other attractions. It is a full, compact, and clear index to the most noteworthy buildings, public works, views, drives, railways, and historical treasures of Boston and its suburbs, and is hardly less useful for residents than for strangers.

The references on the second page of the cover to "BOSTON ILLUSTRATED," call attention to a full Pictorial and Descriptive Hand-Book of the city and its surroundings, which describes and illustrates the topographical, architectural, and historical incidents of Boston and vicinity so fully and concisely as to include within a portable book a vast amount of curious and valuable information respecting the city and its environs. It has been newly revised and brought down to the present year, and is so handsome, useful, and cheap a work, that no one interested in Boston and its history should be without it, while, to all those who intend going farther than Boston, the "HAND-BOOKS OF TRAVEL," noticed on the third page of the cover, will be found useful and valuable companions.

COPYRIGHT, 1875,

BY JAMES R. OSGOOD & CO.

Franklin Press: Rand, Avery, & Co., Boston.

CONTENTS.

HOW TO SEE BOSTON AND THE SUBURBS.
BY HORSE-CARS AND RAILROADS.   PAGE
    The Business Quarter.. 5
    The Back Bay and the Common.............................11
    The South End..13
    South Boston..15
    East Boston 16
    Bunker-Hill District...16
    Cambridge...18
    Chestnut Hill...20
    Roxbury and Dorchester...21
    The Harbor..22
    A Sight from Bunker-Hill Monument.......................22

A SERIES OF DRIVES.
    To Chelsea Beach..25
    To Lexington, Watertown, and Mount Auburn.........25
    To Chestnut Hill and Newton....................................26
    To Jamaica Plain and Forest Hills.............................27
    To Dorchester...27

CONVEYANCES ABOUT BOSTON.
HORSE-RAILROADS.
    Metropolitan Railroad..28
    Highland Railway..32
    South Boston Railroad...33
    Union Railway...34
    Middlesex Railroad..38
    Lynn and Boston Railroad..39
    Citizens' Omnibus Line...40
    Hack Fares..40

CONVEYANCES OUT OF BOSTON.
RAILROADS.
    Fitchburg Railroad...42
    Eastern Railroad..43
    Boston, Lowell, and Nashua Railroad.......................44
    Boston and Maine Railroad..45
    Boston and Providence Railroad................................45
    N. Y. and N. E. Railroad..46
    Boston and Albany Railroad......................................47
    Old Colony Railroad..48

Contents.

STEAMBOATS.
    In the Harbor...49
    Outside..49

MEANS OF COMMUNICATION.
THE POST OFFICE...51

TELEGRAPH OFFICES.
    Western Union..52
    Franklin Telegraph...52

EXPRESSES...52

PLACES OF INTEREST.
    Public Buildings...53
    Statues and Monuments..55
    Parks and Squares..56
    The Principal Wharves..58
    Markets..59
    Libraries..59
    Daily Newspapers...61
    Prominent Churches...61

PLACES OF AMUSEMENT
    Theatres...62
    Music and Lecture Halls......................................63

THE CITY GOVERNMENT FOR 1875.................................65

POLICE DEPARTMENT..66
    Police Stations..66

FIRE DEPARTMENT..66
    Fire Alarms..67

PUBLIC BATHING PLACES..72

HOTELS AND RESTAURANTS.
    Hotels...73
    Restaurants and Cafés..74

NEW POCKET GUIDE

THROUGH

BOSTON AND VICINITY.

How to See Boston and the Suburbs,

BY HORSE-CARS AND RAILROADS.

THIS little book is compiled especially for the use of strangers in Boston, being intended to furnish them with a convenient and compact medium for reference in visiting the various sections of the city, and noting and examining the different objects of interest. Boston is well provided with horse-car facilities, the several lines traversing the entire length of the city, and centering at convenient starting-points in Bowdoin Square, junction of Cambridge, Green, Court, and Chardon Streets; Park Street Church; Temple Place; and in Scollay Square, junction of Tremont, Court, Cornhill, and Pemberton Square. In the following pages will be indicated the routes to be taken by horse-cars, omnibuses, and ferries, or on foot for short distances, and a sketch of a few of the beautiful drives for which the suburbs are famous. The routes mentioned may be taken by those who wish to see Boston and its surroundings in private carriages.

The Business Quarter.

Since the great fire, marked changes have been made in the business section of Boston. In addition to the re-building of the burned district, streets have been extended and widened (but in very few cases straightened), and many new and elegant business edifices take the place of those destroyed in the conflagration. Supposing the visitor to start from Scollay Square, on a pedestrian tour, he should pass down Court Street, noticing on the right the Adams Express Office, the County Court House, and Sears Building, — the latter a very fine edifice, — and on the left two or three handsome granite structures, and the "Daily Advertiser" Building. On reaching Washington Street, turn to the left, and pass down into Dock Square, one of the oldest quarters in the city. Here a great improvement has been made in the extension of Washington Street, which has been cut through to Haymarket Square, and several notable new structures appear, prominent among them being Leopold Morse and Co's. clothing-house; nearly opposite to which is Wilde's Block. A short distance farther in the same direction, and we reach Faneuil Hall, the famous "Cradle of Liberty," surmounted by the grasshopper vane, and, just beyond, the new Faneuil-hall Market, commonly known as Quincy Market. At the lower end of the market, we arrive at Commercial Street, with its elegant and substantial warehouses. Turning to the right, and following Commercial Street, we come to State Street. The granite building in the square is the Custom House; and it will well repay an examination. Facing down the street towards the water, we see the solid and imposing State-street Block of fifteen wide and high stores. Beyond this block is the new marginal Atlan-

ROBERT & GEORGE R. BRINE,

THE GREAT CLOTHIERS,

365 WASHINGTON STREET. 365

Old Number, 201.

tic Avenue, which is to skirt the city on the water side. Facing in the opposite direction, we see the Old State House in the centre of the street, and are looking directly into the square where the famous Boston Massacre took place on March 5, 1770. On either side of the street are business structures, some of them devoted to mercantile purposes, but the most to banking, insurance, lawyers' and brokers' offices, and the like. On the left is the Merchants' Exchange, formerly the Post Office, the latter now forming a conspicuous object on Devonshire, Water and Milk Streets and Post Office Square. We now pass in the rear of the Custom House, into India Street, thence up Milk Street, into Broad, where are situated the principal wholesale grocery establishments. Passing through Broad into Oliver Street, we observe from the variety of new buildings, that we are in the section skirted by the great fire. Here are many metal and hardware establishments. From Oliver we pass into High Street, and enter the Fort Hill District, where a high hill, once covered with dwellings, has been levelled, and the territory devoted to business purposes. We come to Pearl Street, once the headquarters of the shoe trade of this country, and now almost wholly occupied by wholesale boot and shoe dealers. Farther on is Congress Street, to a great extent devoted to the leather interests. And next comes Federal, in the vicinity of which the dealers in wool are largely represented. A few steps farther and we turn into Summer Street, which, rebuilt, presents probably the handsomest appearance of any business street. Passing up the street, we see at the

WM. S. BUTLER & CO.,

90 & 92 TREMONT STREET,

Have the best assortment of

CORSETS

TO BE FOUND IN BOSTON.

corner of Kingston Street the place where the great fire originated, now occupied by handsome buildings. Prominent among the new edifices in this vicinity are the Church Green Block, the Montgomery Building, and the new Bedford Buildings, all of which are very superior specimens of architecture, and are surrounded by other edifices almost equally attractive. We turn into Devonshire Street in order to view Winthrop Square and the central portion of the rebuilt business section of Boston. The square is surrounded by handsome buildings with the Beebe Block as the most prominent among them all. At the corner of Franklin Street is a large iron structure on the site of the old Catholic Cathedral; while just below is the Franklin Building, occupied by James R. Osgood & Co., and Rand, Avery, & Co., and opposite is the Brewer Building, a large and elegant business edifice. Farther up toward Washington Street are numerous business blocks, prominent among which are the granite buildings occupied by Lee & Shepard, L. Prang & Co., &c. We continue our course along Devonshire Street, towards Milk, and are struck by the unique and varied styles of architecture afforded in the newly-erected buildings. At Milk Street we come to the large and stately structure of the Equitable Life Insurance Company, and then to the Rialto Building, surmounted by a dome, and the new Post Office. Looking up Milk Street is seen the office of the Boston Post, on which spot Franklin was born, and the side of the Transcript Building. We pass along by the Devonshire front of the Post Office, till we come to Water Street, and

A. STOWELL & CO.,
IMPORTERS OF

Swiss Crystal,
    Lapsis Lazuli,
        Sicilian Shell,

IN OUR OWN EXCLUSIVE DESIGNS.
16 WINTER STREET.

turn to the right down by the Simmons Building, in order to get a view of Post Office Square, with the new buildings of the Mutual Life Insurance Company of New York, the New England Mutual, and others which may be seen on all sides. The Post Office is to be extended over a portion of the vacant lot on its easterly side. The insurance interests are largely concentrated in the streets around this vicinity. A tour through all the streets of the rebuilt section will richly repay the visitor. In walking, it would be well to take Post Office Square as a starting point, and the way around can easily be found. We will now retrace our steps from Post Office Square up Water Street into Washington, leaving the Old South on the left, and step into School Street, at the northerly corner of which stands the famous Old Corner bookstore. Farther on, at the right hand, we get a view of the magnificent City Hall, in the area in front of which the statue of Franklin keeps guard. Farther up is the ancient King's Chapel, and on the left is the Parker House. On turning to the left into Tremont Street, we find on the right the Tremont House, a large and elegant stone-front hotel of the first class, the Granary Burying Ground, — the third established in Boston, — and Park-street Church. On the left are Tremont Temple, the Horticultural Hall, and the Studio Building. In Winter Street, which comes into Tremont just below the head of the Common, are several dry-goods stores, and the well-known jewelry establishment of A. Stowell & Co. It is a central street for ladies' shopping; and the Music Hall, containing the

THE

NEW ENGLAND ORGAN CO.

MANUFACTURE THE BEST

CABINET ORGAN

FOR THE HOME, CHURCH, OR CHAPEL.

"Great Organ," is on a court just off Winter Street, on the left as one faces Washington Street. Next comes Temple Place, where are some fine business structures. We have meanwhile passed St. Paul's (Episcopal) Church, and the United States Court House, on the corner of Temple Place. Continuing still on Tremont Street, we pass the beautiful marble building occupied by Wm. P. Sargent & Co., and other handsome structures of recent erection, and come to the foot of the Common. Here we see several very fine buildings: on the north-east corner of Tremont and Boylston Streets is the Masonic Temple, dedicated in 1867; on the south-east corner is the Hotel Boylston, one of the most elegant French flat-hotels in the city, owned by the Hon. Charles Francis Adams; on the south-west corner is the Hotel Pelham, the pioneer in Boston of the "flat" system, and famous from having been moved back bodily twenty feet when Tremont Street was widened, without disturbing the occupants of the house; the next building but one, passing down Boylston Street, opposite the Common, is the Public Library, to be mentioned again. Turning now away from the Common into Boylston Street, we reach Washington Street, and, turning to the left, we follow it to Cornhill. On the right we pass the Globe Theatre, and the Emigrant Savings Bank structure. On the left is the Hotel Belmont, while further on is the fine building of the Mercantile Savings Institution and the Boston Theatre. We are now in the great retail district of the city, where may be seen the wholesale and retail dry-goods establishment of

BOATING SHIRTS,

REGATTA SHIRTS,

BATHING TIGHTS, &c., &c.,

AT

BRINE'S,

365   WASHINGTON STREET.   365

Jordan, Marsh, & Co., and the marble building occupied by Macullar, Williams, & Parker's clothing store. Down Washington Street are the Transcript, Journal, Globe, and Herald newspaper offices, and numbers of retail stores of all kinds and descriptions. By turning into Cornhill at Dock Square the visitor soon finds himself in Scollay Square whence he started out on his two-mile ramble.

The Back Bay, Public Garden, and Common.

The section of the city embraced in these three divisions is one of the most attractive offered in Boston, both in extent and variety. To visit the Back Bay, we take a Beacon-street car at the Park-street Church, we pass through Tremont, Boylston, Clarendon, and Marlborough Streets to Dartmouth. Here we are in the region which is now rapidly filling up with elegant dwelling-houses. We leave the car, and pass into Beacon Street, through which we walk to Berkeley Street, between some of the finest mansions in Boston. We walk through Berkeley Street, passing by, first, the very beautiful First Church (Unitarian), then the costly and imposing Central Church (Cong. Trin.). Between the two is Commonwealth Avenue, already a fine street, but one that will be still more delightful when it has been extended, as is designed, to Brookline, and when the rows of trees shall have attained greater size. We pass also, beyond, the Central Church, and the fine building of the Boston Society of Natural History, which is open to the public every Wednes-

Customers can fill their memorandum in every thing in the

SMALL WARE LINE

AT

WM. S. BUTLER & CO.,

90 & 92 Tremont Street.

day and Saturday. We must turn down Boylston Street to see its companion building the Massachusetts Institute of Technology. In this vicinity, too, one can get an excellent idea of the magnitude of the Back Bay improvements. Taking his station at the junction of Boylston and Dartmouth, with his back to Beacon Street, he sees on the right the splendid edifice of the Old South Society; on the left, the new Chauncy-Hall School; while in front, near where Huntingdon Avenue joins Boylston Street, are seen the new Museum of Fine Arts, and the new buildings of the Trinity Church Society. The square tower of the Brattle-street Church, with its numerous figures, forms an attractive object at the corner of Commonwealth Avenue and Clarendon Street, and the four or five handsome family hotels in this vicinity may be easily distinguished from their peculiar dimensions and architecture. Retracing our steps, we pass up Boylston Street to Arlington, where we turn to the left, and walk on the Public-Garden side of the street, the better to see the Arlington-street Church and the magnificent residences on the westerly side, to the central gate of the Garden. On entering the Public Garden we find ourselves facing Ball's excellent equestrian statue of Washington. To the left we see a group of statuary representing the Good Samaritan, on a pedestal, — the noble gift of a private citizen, to adorn these grounds, and to commemorate the discovery of anæsthetics. Beyond, at the centre of the northerly side, we see the statue of Edward Everett. We cross the bridge, and pass directly through the Garden, unless we prefer to

A. STOWELL & CO.,

16 WINTER STREET,

IMPORTERS OF

FINE SILK AND SATIN FANS

IN ALL THEIR VARIOUS COMBINATIONS.

Paris Fans, Vienna Fans, Opera Glasses.

wander about, or to rest upon one of the seats so abundantly provided; and, crossing Charles Street, we are in the Common. Here is occupation for many a leisure hour. We may enjoy the spectacle of the boys at their sport on the Parade Ground; we may wander up to the Boylston-street side, and look into the ancient graveyard or the pleasant deer-park; we may climb the hill, and see the foundation of the Soldiers' Monument; we may sit down by the Frog Pond, and watch the boys and girls at play; we may go and see the famous Old Elm, which has been a living tree since Boston was first settled, and from whose branches more than one supposed witch has been suspended; or we may walk idly along the broad malls in the refreshing shade of the grand old trees. We should not fail, however, to see, before our return to Park-street Church, the fine bronze fountain near the Park-street mall, which the generosity of a single citizen has placed there. Nor could the tour end more profitably than by a visit to the State House, where scores of interesting objects are to be seen, and by climbing to the cupola, from which the best view of Boston is to be had.

The South End.

Our next trip is one that can be made mostly by horse-cars, and calls for but a small exercise of pedestrian powers. We will start, as before, from Park-street Church, taking a Lenox-street car, and riding to its southern terminus. We pass over familiar ground to Boylston Street, but continue in

I consider the Cabinet Organs manufactured by the

NEW ENGLAND ORGAN COMPANY

fully equal in tone, mechanism, and appearance to those produced in any establishment in the country; and would call attention to the "soft register," or Dulciana, as being uncommonly delicate and refined.

JOHN H. WILLCOX, Mus. Doc.

Tremont Street to the South End. After crossing the bridge over the Boston and Albany Railroad, we pass on the right, the extensive Bay-State Moulding Mills. Beyond Berkeley Street, on the corner of which is the elegant new Odd Fellows' Hall, we come into the region of churches. On the right is the Clarendon-street Baptist Church, close by the Smith American Organ Factory. On the left are the peculiar-shaped brick tower of the Shawmut Congregational Church, and the beautiful structure of the Tremont-street Methodist Society. Arrived at the end of our route, we notice the immense factory where Chickering's piano-fortes are made. We pass through Northampton Street northward to Columbus Avenue, merely to glance at that fine thoroughfare, from the extreme end of which we see the steeple of Park-street Church, and to pass up one block to West Chester Park. We walk through the latter avenue and Chester Square to Washington Street. One block northward on Washington Street brings us to the marble-front Commonwealth Hotel. Another block, and we come to Worcester Square on the right-hand side. We pass through Worcester Square to Harrison Avenue, having in front of us the immense City Hospital. Turning down Harrison Avenue, we come at Concord Street to the Church of the Immaculate Conception, and Boston College. At Newton Street we turn once more towards Washington Street, but pass into Franklin Square, in order the better to examine the imposing front of the St. James Hotel. On the opposite side of Washington Street is the mate to Franklin Square,—

HOME-SPUN PANTS

MADE TO ORDER FOR

$8.00 and $10.00,

AT

BRINE'S,

365 *WASHINGTON STREET.* *365*

Blackstone Square. A short distance down Washington Street, we come to the yet unfinished but majestic Cathedral of the Holy Cross. On the left, and a little farther on is the Continental Hotel, — an immense and very elegant marble-front hotel on the French flat system. We may now take any horse-car that overtakes us and arrive back at Park-street Church, after passing on the way many objects of interest, which it is unnecessary to specify. Another trip to the South End and Highlands, through Tremont Street, Shawmut Avenue, &c., is offered by the cars of the Highland Railway.

South Boston.

There are several public buildings in South Boston that should be visited if time permit. We may take a car marked "South Boston, Broadway," at Scollay Square, and pass at first through a district we have already visited. In Summer Street we see many fine business houses that we have not previously included in our trips. In Chauncy Street we see many large dry-goods houses, and pass on the right the fine building of the Massachusetts Charitable Mechanic Association, which is occupied by the Boston and the National Boards of Trade. On our route we pass by the United States Hotel, and the stations of the Albany and the Old Colony Railroads. We are supposed to have provided ourselves at the head-quarters of the Institution for the Blind, No. 20 Bromfield Street, with permits to enter that asylum, and we soon arrive on the Heights where it is situated. The

At 90 & 92 Tremont Street, may be found a full line of Straw Goods at the very lowest prices,

WM. S. BUTLER & CO.

visit cannot fail to be exceedingly interesting. After leaving the Institution, we walk through Broadway and M Streets, by Independence Square, to the territory occupied by the House of Correction, House of Industry, Insane Hospital, and Almshouse. Returning to the corner of K Street and Broadway, we take a Bay-View and Eighth-street car into the city by another route.

East Boston.

The principal objects of interest in East Boston are the Grand Junction Wharves and the Cunard Steamer Docks. We start once more from Scollay Square by an East-Boston car, and pass through the poorest quarter of the city, — the Five Points of Boston. After a pleasant trip across the ferry, we are landed very near the Grand-Junction Wharves, which we reach by passing through Marginal Street. Cunard Wharf lies directly on the way, and we shall be peculiarly unfortunate if we do not see one of the great ocean freight steamers at the dock or lying in the stream. The scene on the arrival of one of these steamers, when she is discharging her cargo or reloading, is full of interest; and the busy activity of the Grand-Junction Wharves at all times makes this one of the trips that ought to be taken.

Bunker Hill District.

We will make the circuit of the suburban towns, beginning on the North. Charlestown, or as it is called since annexation, "The Bunker Hill District,"

TORTOISE SHELL JEWELRY,

Necklaces, Lockets, Brooches,

EARRINGS and PENDANTS,

Imported and Domestic Styles and Patterns.

ALL NEW DESIGNS IN COMBS.

is reached by any car of the Middlesex Railroad; but we will take a Chelsea car, of the Lynn and Boston Railroad, that will carry us by the Navy Yard. On our way we pass by the Boston and Maine Railroad Station in Haymarket Square, and over Charles-river Bridge into Charlestown Square, where we shall see the building, once a fine hotel, known as the Waverley, which was built out of the profits of the "Waverley Magazine," but is now used for various business purposes. Arrived at the Navy Yard, we leave the car, and examine the numerous points of interest within. On leaving the yard, we shall see the tall shaft of Bunker-hill Monument, and shall need no guide to direct us to it. We must of course climb the monument, and obtain one of the finest views to be had anywhere. From the south window we have a complete bird's-eye view of Boston; from the east, the harbor; from the north, Everett, Chelsea, Revere, Malden, and Lynn; and from the west window we look out to Cambridge and Arlington, to Watertown and Belmont; and in a clear day we may see Wachusett Mountain in Worcester County, and Kearsarge and the White Mountains in New Hampshire. The several points to be noticed are briefly described elsewhere. From the monument, we should pass near enough to the State Prison, at least to see its gloomy and forbidding walls; and a walk into the city from that point will not be a great task. If, after crossing by the lower or Charles-river Bridge, we pass down Commercial Street a short distance, we shall be in the immediate vicinity of the ancient Copp's-hill Burying Ground, between Snowhill and

THE NEW ENGLAND CABINET ORGAN.

THE FAVORITE INSTRUMENT FOR THE HOME CIRCLE.

Illustrated Catalogue sent on application.

Hull Streets: that will well repay a visit. We then pass through Hull Street to Salem Street, by Christ Church, — the oldest church-building yet remaining in the city. From Salem Street we pass into Hanover, and through that formerly narrow but now spacious street, past the American House, — the largest hotel in the city, — on the right, into Court Street and Scollay Square, whence we started.

Cambridge.

In order to see as much as possible of Cambridge in one trip, we will take at Bowdoin Square, opposite the Revere House, a car marked "East Cambridge, Harvard Square." We pass through Green and Leverett Streets, and cross Craigie's Bridge. In East Cambridge we see a large number of important factories. We pass through Cambridge Street, its whole length, to Harvard Square, where we alight, and inspect the old and new buildings of Harvard College. In coming to the Square through Cambridge Street, we have passed, first, Appleton Chapel, in the corner of the college yard; then Holworthy Hall, built with money raised by a lottery: Thayer, Stoughton, and Hollis, all dormitories. We now see, close to the fence, Harvard Hall with its belfry, and directly opposite old Massachusetts Hall, built in the seventeenth century, the oldest building in the yard, having a clock-face that was put up in 1725. In the corner nearest to Brattle Street are Grays, Matthews, and Wells Halls; and a little beyond, on Harvard Street, is Boylston Hall, where is deposited

BARGAINS IN

HOSIERY, UNDERWEAR, NECK WEAR,

AT

BRINE'S,

365 *WASHINGTON STREET.* *365*

the College Museum: that may be visited. Boylston Hall may be recognized from its being the only rough-granite building in the yard. A short distance beyond, and farther removed from the street, is Gore Hall, where is the rich old library of the university, — a building which is also open to the public. The buildings of the Lawrence Scientific School, the Divinity School, the Museum of Comparative Zoölogy, and the Memorial Hall, are outside the college yard, between Cambridge and Kirkland Streets, and beyond Kirkland Street. After having inspected these several buildings, we take a Garden Street and Mount Auburn car. We pass by the Common, with the Soldiers' Monument on the right, and by the elegant new church of the Shepherd Congregational Society on the left. In the middle of the street is the famous Washington Elm, under which Gen. Washington took command of the American army in 1775. At Mount Auburn we pass into that great city of the dead, where again we shall find occupation for all the time that can be spared. No one should fail to visit the chapel, and to ascend to the top of the tower. In returning we take a Mount Auburn car that is not marked "Garden Street," and we shall then return through Brattle Street to Harvard Square. On our way we pass by the residence of the poet Longfellow, — an old mansion of the Revolutionary period, used in 1775 by Gen. Washington as his headquarters. On our way into the city through Main Street, we see a great many fine residences and churches; and from West Boston Bridge we get another excellent view of Boston, especially the Back-bay region. It will be

DON'T FORGET

to visit the NEW STORE of

COOLIDGE, SMITH & CO.,

70 & 72 Tremont Street,

for all kinds of

MILLINERY GOODS.

well to finish up our views in Boston proper, by leaving the car at Charles Street, just after crossing the bridge; and turning to the left near the Mason & Hamlin Cabinet Organ Factory, we shall soon come to the City Jail, a fine granite building. A little farther on we see the magnificent building of the Massachusetts General Hospital: we pass up Allen Street, and then, turning to the right, pass through Chambers to Cambridge Street. Ascending Cambridge Street, we see on the left the old building of the West Church. Nearly opposite is Temple Street, up which we walk, past Grace Church on the right, to the massive stone Beacon-hill Reservoir. This solid structure now stands where was the highest point of Beacon Hill before it was cut down. We go over the hill, and through Mount Vernon Street to Beacon Street. Turning to the left, we soon reach the Boston Athenæum, where is a fine gallery of paintings on exhibition, and a very large library, which may be visited. On leaving the Athenæum, we pass through Beacon and Somerset Streets and Pemberton Square, — a nest of lawyers', architects', and corporation offices, — to Scollay Square.

Chestnut Hill.

We follow our plan of describing routes to be taken by those who wish to see the leading points of interest in and about Boston without incurring the expense of a private carriage. Nevertheless, it must be said that the drive to Chestnut Hill is one of the most charming imaginable; and if one drive, and

---

A. STOWELL & CO.,
DEALERS IN

Gold Jewelry and Silver Ware,
Clocks, Bronzes, Fancy Goods,
RUSSIA LEATHER GOODS,
FANS, OPERA GLASSES, &c.,
16 WINTER STREET.

one only, is to be taken by the visitor to Boston, this should certainly be chosen in preference to all others. The cheaper conveyance, however, is by the steam-cars. A train of the Boston, Hartford, and Erie Railroad should be taken at the Boston and Albany Station, and a ticket purchased for Chestnut Hill. The train will stop at several points of interest along the way; but these need not be described. Nor need any thing be said of the most lovely views at Chestnut Hill itself. If the visitor has driven to the Reservoir, he will find numerous ways of returning to the city different from that by which he went out; but the less extravagant traveller must return by the railroad.

Roxbury and Dorchester.

The horse-car routes through these new wards of Boston are so arranged, and the objects of interest are so far distant from each other, that, if one wishes simply to see the sights of Boston, he must occupy a great deal of time. We shall therefore in this place merely indicate the routes to be taken to each particular point, leaving each one to decide which of them, if not all, he will see. Forest-hills Cemetery is reached by the Forest-hills horse-cars, which start from Park-street Church. The cemetery lies in the West Roxbury district, and in reaching it we pass through an interesting part of Roxbury. If we take a Dorchester and Grove-hall car, also from Park-street Church, we shall pass, on Warren Street, in Roxbury, the estate of Gen. Joseph Warren, who fell at Bunker Hill; and, after noticing on either

---

I consider the Cabinet Organs manufactured by the

NEW ENGLAND ORGAN COMPANY

fully equal in tone, mechanism, and appearance to those produced in any establishment in the country; and would call attention to the "soft register," or Dulciana, as being uncommonly delicate and refined.

JOHN H. WILLCOX, Mus. Doc.

side the elegant estates and fine residences which line Warren Street, we come to Grove Hall, now occupied for a Consumptives' Home. The Mount Pleasant cars will carry us to a beautiful part of Roxbury; and near the terminus of the line is the estate of Gov. Eustis, with its ample grounds and spacious residence. Dorchester is very beautiful in many parts; and the horse-cars, which start from the foot of Summer Street, or the Old Colony and the Hartford and Erie Railroads, will carry one to almost any desired point.

The Harbor.

A visit to Boston should not be considered as finished before one has taken a sail down the harbor. There are several routes that may be followed; and it would be difficult to choose among them, since they all afford an opportunity to see nearly every point of interest in this part of the suburbs. They all take one past the forts and among the islands, give a view of the surrounding country, and whether running to Long Island, to Hull, to Downer's Landing, to Strawberry Hill, to Nantasket Beach, to Hingham, or to Nahant, reach some point that will, by its beauty and the interest that attaches to it, well repay a visit.

A Sight from Bunker-hill Monument.

It is so difficult to identify familiar objects from a new point of view, that it is well to have some assistance in looking over such a vast expanse of country

---

UMBRELLAS,

    SLEEVE BUTTONS,

        SCARF RINGS, &c., &c.,

AT

BRINE'S,

365   WASHINGTON STREET.   365

as is opened to our view from the top of Bunker-hill Monument. We will suppose the visitor to the monument to look out first to the north. We notice, first, the singular peninsula of Nahant, with its long neck reaching to Lynn, the city of shoes; and then we follow the coast across the mouth of Saugus River, along Revere or Chelsea Beach, to the little town of Winthrop. To the left of the coast, we see the city of Chelsea spread out before us; the towns of Malden, Everett, Melrose, and Saugus, with their numerous villages; and the trains on the Eastern and the Boston and Maine Roads passing along their swift but apparently snail-like course.

We turn now to the west, and here a glorious prospect opens before us. The entire country is dotted with villages, crossed by railroads, watered by rivers, made beautiful by being covered with pretty and comfortable dwelling-houses. On the extreme right, we see close beneath our feet the new city of Somerville; and Medford lies beyond it. Turning a little to the left, we look out over Arlington towards Lexington; and, if it be a clear day, we may see the White Mountains from this point; while due west we see Cambridge, the University, the United States Arsenal in Watertown, and Mount Auburn.

A little farther south we see Brighton and its stock-yards; the beautiful town of Newton, — formerly a cluster of pretty villages, but rapidly becoming an area wholly covered by one great village; Brookline, with its reservoir; beyond, the Chestnut-hill Reservoir; and a little more to the south, Jamaica Pond.

WM. S. BUTLER & CO.,

90 & 92 TREMONT STREET.

THE LARGEST AND BEST ASSORTMENT OF

MILLINERY GOODS

TO BE FOUND IN BOSTON.

Once more we change our position, and look out of the south window upon Boston. The sight is at first somewhat confusing. We see a vast area completely covered with dwellings, churches, and warehouses. Only the practised eye can pick out any particular building that differs but slightly from the rest in architecture. We shall have no difficulty in finding the State House. Close to it is the First Baptist Church on Somerset Street. We can see the peculiar steeple of the Old South to the left; and the churches on the Back Bay may be easily distinguished. From this station we may see the line of every railroad out of Boston. Roxbury and Dorchester, now constituting four of the wards of Boston, lie beyond the city proper; and at the extreme left we may see, on Dorchester Heights in South Boston, the Perkins Institution for the Blind, and beyond, several city institutions, which are only pleasant objects to look at when visited voluntarily.

We look out now from the east window upon the harbor and East Boston. Forts Winthrop and Independence lie comparatively near, and will easily be distinguished. Upon Long-Island Head we see the lighthouse that has been erected to guide vessels into the inner harbor. Farther down the harbor is the famous Fort Warren, and beyond it the town of Hull. If the weather is clear, we may see, at the entrance of the harbor, the outer Boston Light. Nearly beneath our eyes lies East Boston; and we may easily distinguish the extensive wharves and grain elevator of the Boston and Albany Railroad, and the wharf where the Cunard steamers land their passengers and cargo.

A. STOWELL & CO.,
16 WINTER STREET,

IMPORTERS OF

Fans,
    Chatelaines,
        Opera Glasses,
            Hair Ornaments,
Tortoise Shell Combs,
    Imitation Shell Combs,
        Bisc Flower Sets,
            Roman Pearl Knobs, etc.

A SERIES OF DRIVES.

To Chelsea Beach.

An interesting drive for visitors from the interior, to whom the sight of the sea is a novelty, may be laid out as follows : starting from any central point, — as, for instance, Scollay Square, — we will proceed through Hanover, Union, and Charlestown Streets, over Charles-river Bridge, to Charlestown. We then pay a visit to Bunker-hill Monument and the Navy Yard on our way, and proceed over Chelsea Bridge to Chelsea; thence directly through the city to Revere Village, where we turn to the right, and ride down to Revere or Chelsea Beach. This is a magnificent beach, smooth and hard, upon which the waves dash grandly. The Highland Park Hotel, on "Powderhorn Hill," is a new summer resort; and from it a fine view of surrounding scenery is obtained. In returning, we may come back by way of Everett, Malden, Medford, and the new city of Somerville, seeing how rapidly the suburbs of Boston are growing, and entering the city by way of Craigie's Bridge, through East Cambridge.

To Lexington, Watertown, and Mount Auburn.

The easiest way to visit the battle-ground of Lexington is by railroad; still it may be reached by a rather long but very interesting drive. We pass out of Boston by the West Boston (Cambridge) Bridge, and, taking Broadway, follow the direct road through

THE NEW ENGLAND CABINET ORGAN.

THE FAVORITE INSTRUMENT FOR THE HOME CIRCLE.

Illustrated Catalogue sent on application.

Cambridge, past Fresh Pond, into and through Arlington, into Lexington. Turning then to the north, we ride through East Lexington Village to Lexington Village and the battle-field, on which may be seen the new statues of Hancock and Adams. On our return, we visit Waltham, where the great American Watch Factory is situated, and, passing through Newton into Watertown, stop to look over the United States Arsenal; thence to Mount Auburn, by the houses of Lowell and Longfellow, and the Washington Elm, to Harvard Square and the buildings of the University, elsewhere described, and thence back to Boston.

To Chestnut Hill and Newton.

This is the favorite direction for drives out of Boston. The route is by way of Beacon Street, through the whole length of that magnificent avenue, and over the Milldam Road. On reaching the fork in the road, we take the branch to the right, — Brighton Avenue, — and continue to the Baptist Church at the corner of Cambridge Street. We have been passing over the "Brighton Road," famed in song, and the popular sleigh-drive on the few occasions in winter when that class of vehicles can be brought into use. We turn now to the left, and pass through Brighton to Newton Corner, thence by Centre Street to Newton Centre, where we take Beacon Street, and return by the way of the Chestnut-hill Reservoir, and from thence in a straight line, by Corey's Hill, into Boston by the way we went out.

CUSTOM DEPARTMENT.

Garments made to order in the best style, and at lower prices than any other house in the city.

"*FOR CASH ONLY.*"

ROBERT & GEORGE R. BRINE,

365 WASHINGTON STREET. 365

To Jamaica Plain and Forest Hills.

Our next drive is to the suburbs on the south of the city; and, as before, we will make a circuit. Passing once more out of the city by Beacon Street and the Milldam Road, we take the left branch, and pass through Western Avenue, and the beautiful village of Longwood, to the Brookline Reservoir on Boylston Street. From the reservoir, by a winding road that gives us some glimpses of lovely scenery, we come to the charming Jamaica Pond, around which we ride; thence to Forest-hills Cemetery, and back into Boston by way of Shawmut Avenue, Egleston Square, Walnut Avenue, Warren Street, and Washington Street.

To Dorchester.

Our last suburban drive takes us through the greater part of Roxbury and Dorchester. We ride through Tremont Street and Shawmut Avenue, to Dudley Street, then through Warren Street, past the Warren House, to Grove Hall, and by way of Bluehill Avenue, to Mattapan Village, and the Blue Hills in Milton. Returning, we ride through Milton Lower Mills, Harrison Square, Savin Hill, and South Boston, passing by the Blind Asylum, if we wish, over the Federal-street Bridge, into the city.

COOLIDGE, SMITH, & CO.,
70 & 72 TREMONT STREET.

NEW STORE AND NEW GOODS.
Hosiery, Gloves, Straw Goods,
FLOWERS, RIBBONS, &c., &c.

CONVEYANCES ABOUT BOSTON.

HORSE-RAILROAD.

Metropolitan Railroad.

This company serves all the North, West, and South Ends of Boston, Brookline, West Roxbury, Roxbury, a part of Dorchester, a part of South Boston, and East Boston. It has a large number of routes, which are in detail as follows: —

Boston Neck and Depot Cars. — Inward trips, from the corner of Washington and Camden Streets, through Washington, Temple Place, Tremont, Court, Green, Leverett, and Causeway Streets, to the Fitchburg-railroad Station. Outward trips, from Fitchburg-railroad Station, through Causeway, Portland, Chardon, Court, Cornhill, Washington, Summer, Chauncy, Harrison Avenue, East Dover, and Washington Streets, to corner of Camden.

Boston Neck and Charles-Street Cars. — Inward trips, from corner of Washington and Camden Streets, through Washington, Temple Place, Tremont, Court, Green, Chambers, Cambridge, and Charles Streets, to Boylston Street. Outward trips, back through Charles, Cambridge, Court, Cornhill, Washington, Summer, Chauncy, Harrison Avenue, East Dover, and Washington Streets, to Camden Street.

Boston Neck and Chelsea-Ferry Cars. — Inward trips, from corner of Camden and Washington Streets by route of the depot cars, to corner of Court and

---

A. STOWELL & CO.,
BOSTON.
ROMAN GOLD NECKLACES,
Lockets, Pendants, and Crosses,
14Kt. WATCH CHAINS AND GENTLEMEN'S SEALS.
16 Winter Street.

Hanover Streets, thence through Hanover Street to Chelsea Ferry. Outward trips, through Hanover Street to New Washington, to Summer, Chauncy, &c., to Camden Street.

Mount Pleasant Cars. — Inward trips, from Mount Pleasant Station, through Dudley, Dearborn, Eustis, Washington, Temple Place, and Tremont Streets, to Scollay Square. Outward trips, back through Court, Washington, Summer, Chauncy, Harrison Avenue, East Dover, Washington, Eustis, Dearborn, and Dudley Streets, to station.

Warren-Street Cars. — Inward trips, from corner of Warren and Maywood Streets, through Warren, Washington, Temple Place, and Tremont Streets, to depots. Outward trips, back, through Causeway, Portland, Chardon, to Bowdoin Square; then by depot-car line to Warren Street.

Dorchester and Grove-Hall Cars. — From Washington Street, Dorchester District, near old Town Hall, through Washington and Warren Streets, and thence to Tremont House by route of Warren-street cars. Outward trips, by Tremont, West Dover, and Washington Streets, to Warren.

Norfolk House Cars. — Round trips, starting from Norfolk House, Eliot Square, through Dudley, Washington, Temple Place, Tremont, Cornhill, Washington, to the depots. Outward trips from the Depots, through Merrimac, Washington Street, Harrison Avenue, East Dover and Washington Streets, to starting point.

Egleston-Square Cars. — Inward trips, from corner of Egleston Square and Washington Street, through

THE NEW ENGLAND ORGAN CO.,
MANUFACTURERS OF

CABINET ORGANS.

OFFICE AND WAREROOMS, 1299 Washington St.,
MANUFACTORY, 49, 51, 53, 55, 57, & 59 Wareham St.,
BOSTON.

Washington Street, Temple Place, and **Tremont** Streets, to Tremont House. Outward trips, from Tremont House, back through Tremont, West Dover, and Washington Streets, to Egleston Square.

Forest-Hills Cars. — Inward trips, from Forest-hills Station, through Washington Street, and the route of Egleston-square cars, to the Tremont House. Outward trips, by route of Egleston-square cars, extended to Forest-hills Station.

Lenox-Street Cars. — Inward trips, from corner of Tremont and Lenox Streets, through Tremont Street to the Tremont House. Outward trips, back, through Tremont Street, to Lenox Street.

Lenox-Street and Depot Cars. — Inward trips, from corner of Lenox and Tremont Streets, through Tremont, Berkeley, Boylston, Tremont, Court, Green, Leverett, and Causeway Streets, to Fitchburg-railroad Station. Outward trips, back, through Causeway, Portland, Chardon, Court, Cornhill, Washington, Temple Place, Tremont, Boylston, Berkeley, and Tremont Streets, to Lenox Street.

Tremont-Street Cars. — Inward trips, from crossing of Tremont Street and Providence Railroad, through Tremont Street, to Tremont House. Outward trips, back, through Tremont Street, to Station.

Jamaica Plain (West Roxbury) Cars. — Inward trips, from Jamaica Plain, through Austin, Centre, Pynchon, and Tremont Streets, to the Tremont House. Outward trips, back over the same route.

Brookline Cars. — Inward trips, from Harvard Square, Brookline, through Roxbury Street (Brook-

---

BLACK CLOTH VESTS.

Single Breast $1.75, $2.00
Double Breast $2.50

—AT—

BRINE'S,

365 **WASHINGTON STREET.** *365*

line) and Tremont Street, to Tremont House. Outward trips, back over the same route.

Beacon-Street Cars. — Round trips, from corner of Parker and Marlboro' Streets, through Marlboro', Clarendon, Boylston, and Tremont Streets, to Tremont House. Outward trips, return by same route.

East Boston Cars. — Inward trips from Bartlett Street, Highlands, through Washington Street, Temple Place, Tremont, Hanover, and Battery Streets to the North Ferry. Thence by ferry to East Boston side, where another car may be taken through Sumner Street, Maverick Square, and Meridian Street, to Eutaw Street. Return by same route to the ferry, taking a car on the other side through Battery, Hanover, and New Washington, Summer, Chauncy, Harrison Avenue, and Washington, to Bartlett-street station. No cars cross the East Boston Ferry, but tickets are good to the end of the route.

Dudley-Street Depot Cars. — Inward trips from Bartlett Street, Highlands, through Washington, Temple Place, Tremont, Cornhill, New Washington, Haymarket Square, Boston and Maine Depot, and Haverhill Street, to Fitchburg, Eastern, and Lowell Depots. Outward trips through Portland, Merrimac, New Washington, following ferry and depot lines, to Dudley Street.

Upham's Corner Cars. — Inward trips from Upham's Corner, Dorchester District, through Stoughton, Dudley, Dearborn, Eustis, Washington Street, and Temple Place, to Tremont House. Outward trips from Tremont House through Tremont, West Dover, and Washington Street, following Mt. Pleasant route,

JAPANESE FANS,

Silk Fans, Autograph Fans, Feather Fans,

OF ALL KINDS AND PRICES, AT

WILLIAM S. BUTLER & CO.'S,

90 & 92 TREMONT STREET.

extended to Upham's Corner, connecting with Dorchester-avenue Road.

Meeting-house-hill Cars. — Inward trips, from Meeting-house-hill, via Upton's Corner, Mt. Pleasant to Washington Street, Temple Place to Tremont House. Outward trips, by Upham's Corner route.

Field's-Corner Cars. — Inward trips, from crossing of Adams and Hancock Streets with Dorchester Avenue (Dorchester), through Dorchester Avenue and Federal Street, to foot of Summer Street. Outward trips, back over the same route.

Highland Railway.

Grove-Hall Cars. — Inward trips from Grove Hall, junction of Warren Street and Bluehill Avenue, through Warren, Dudley, Shawmut Avenue, Tremont (after 6, P.M., to Scollay Square), Eliot, and Washington Streets, to Temple Place. Outward trips from Temple Place, through Tremont Street, Shawmut Avenue, Dudley, Street to Grove Hall over inward route.

Dudley-Street Cars. — Inward trips from Dudley-street office, through Dudley Street, Shawmut Avenue, Tremont, Eliot, and Washington Streets, to Temple Place. Return to Dudley Street over route of Grove-hall cars.

Warren-Street Cars. — Inward trips from Warren Street, corner Woodbine, through Warren, Dudley, Shawmut Avenue, Tremont, to Scollay Square. Out-

---

A. STOWELL & Co.

IMPORTERS OF

Special Novelties in Fancy Jewelry,

GILT, JET, SHELL, OXYDIZED, ETC.

FANS! FANS! FANS!

16 WINTER STREET.

ward trips through Cornhill, Washington Street, Temple Place, Tremont, Shawmut Avenue, Dudley, and Warren Streets, to station.

Mount-Pleasant Cars. — Inward trips from Bluehill Avenue, corner of Dennis Street, through Bluehill Avenue, Dudley Street, Shawmut Avenue, and Tremont Street, to Scollay Square. Outward trips through Cornhill, Washington Streets, Temple Place, Tremont Street, Shawmut Avenue, Dudley Street, and Bluehill Avenue, to station.

South-Boston Railroad.

South Boston Cars. — Inward trips, from the office of the company, corner of K Street and Broadway, through Broadway, Emerson, Third, Dorchester, Broadway, Federal, Kneeland, South, Beach, Washington, Boylston, and Tremont Streets, to Scollay Square. Outward trips, from Scollay Square, through Cornhill, Washington, Summer, Chauncy, Harrison Avenue, Beach, Federal, Broadway, Dorchester, Third, Emerson, and Broadway, to office of the company.

Broadway Cars. — Inward trips, from office of company, through Broadway to Federal, thence into Boston proper by the route of the South Boston line. Outward trips, from Scollay Square, by route of South Boston cars, to Broadway, thence through Broadway to the station.

City Point Cars. — Inward trips, from City Point, through Fourth, L, and Emerson Streets, and the route of the South Boston cars, into Boston proper.

THE

NEW ENGLAND ORGAN CO.

EMPLOY THE

MOST SKILFUL WORKMEN

IN PRODUCING THEIR

UNRIVALLED CABINET ORGANS.

Outward trips, from Scollay Square, by route of the South Boston cars, thence, by Broadway, L, and Fourth Streets, to City Point.

Bay View and Eighth-Street Cars. — Inward trips, from corner of K and Broadway, through K, Eighth, E, Sixth, C, Fourth, and Federal, to Kneeland, thence inward, by the route of the South-Boston cars. Outward trips, from Scollay Square, by the route of the South Boston cars, to Federal, thence, by inward route of the Bay View cars, to the office of the company.

Union Railway.

This company's cars run to all parts of Cambridge, and to Watertown, Brighton, Arlington, and Somerville. It has nearly twenty routes, which are in detail as follows. To save repetitions, it may be remarked, that outside of Boston the inward and outward routes are the same, and that the starting-point of all the cars in Boston is Bowdoin Square.

Prospect-Street (Cambridgeport) Cars. — Inward trips, from corner of Prospect and Main Streets, Cambridge, through Main Street, West Boston Bridge, and Cambridge Street, to Bowdoin Square. Outward trips, through Green, Chambers, and Cambridge Streets, West Boston Bridge and Main Street, to the station.

Riverside-Press Cars. — Inward trips, from Riverside Press, foot of River Street, through River and Main Streets, West Boston Bridge, and Cambridge Street, to Bowdoin Square. Outward trips, through

---

WE MAKE A SPECIALTY OF

NEW YORK CLOTHING.

ROBERT & GEORGE R. BRINE,

365   WASHINGTON STREET.   365

Green, Chambers, and Cambridge Streets, West Boston Bridge, Main, and River Streets, to station.

Brighton Cars. — Inward trips, from Brighton village, through Cambridge Street (Brighton), River, and Main Streets, West Boston Bridge, and Cambridge Street, to Bowdoin Square. Outward trips, through Green, Chambers and Cambridge Streets, West Boston Bridge, and thence by inward route.

Harvard-Square Cars. — Inward trips, from Harvard Square (Cambridge), through Harvard and Main Streets, West Boston Bridge, and Cambridge Street, to Bowdoin Square. Outward trips, through Green, Chambers, and Cambridge Streets, and thence by inward route.

Mount Auburn (Garden-Street) Cars. — From Mount Auburn, near the railroad station, through Brattle Street, Concord Avenue, Garden Street, North Avenue, Harvard Square, Harvard and Main Streets, West Boston Bridge, and Cambridge Street, to Bowdoin Square. Outward trips, through Green, Chambers, and Cambridge Streets, and thence by inward route.

Mount Auburn Cars. — Inward trips, from Mount Auburn (same station), through Brattle Street to Harvard Square, thence into Boston by route of Harvard-square line. Outward trips, through Green, Chambers, and Cambridge Streets, and thence by inward route.

Watertown Cars. — Inward trips, from Watertown Village, through Pleasant, Mount Auburn, and Brattle Streets, to Harvard Square, thence into Boston by

WM. S. BUTLER & CO.,

90 & 92 TREMONT STREET,

Have the best assortment of

CORSETS

TO BE FOUND IN BOSTON.

route of Harvard-square line. Outward trips, through Green, Chambers, and Cambridge Streets, and thence by inward route.

North Avenue (Rice-Street) Cars. — Inward trips, from corner of Rice Street and North Avenue, through North Avenue, to Harvard Square, thence into Boston by route of the Harvard-square line. Outward trips, through Green, Chambers, and Cambridge Streets, and thence by inward route.

Arlington Cars. — Inward trips, from Arlington Village, through Arlington and North Avenue, to Harvard Square, thence into Boston by route of Harvard-square line. Outward trips, through Green, Chambers, and Cambridge Streets, and thence by inward route.

Broadway (Inman-Street) Cars. — Inward trips, from corner of Broadway and Inman Streets (Cambridge), through Broadway, West Boston Bridge, and Cambridge Street, to Bowdoin Square. Outward trips, through Green, Chambers, and Cambridge Streets, West Boston Bridge, and Broadway, to corner of Inman Street.

Broadway (Harvard-Square) Cars. — Inward trips, from Harvard Square, through Harvard Square, Cambridge Street, Broadway, West Boston Bridge, and Cambridge Street, to Bowdoin Square. Outward trips, through Green, Chambers, and Cambridge Streets, West-Boston Bridge, and Broadway, to Harvard Square.

Eighth Street (East Cambridge) Cars.— Inward trips, from corner of Eighth and Cambridge Streets, East Cambridge, through Cambridge and Bridge Streets,

---

A. STOWELL & CO.,

16 Winter Street,

Importers of Fine French Marble Clocks,

CHOICE BRONZE,

VIENNA FANCY GOODS.

Craigie's Bridge, Leverett, Brighton, Lowell, Causeway, Portland, and Chardon Streets, to Bowdoin Square. Outward trips, through Green and Leverett Streets, Craigie's Bridge, and Cambridge Streets, to station.

Atwood's Corner (East Cambridge) Cars. — Inward trips, from corner of Beacon, Hampshire, and Cambridge Streets, through Cambridge and Bridge Streets, Craigie's Bridge, and thence to Bowdoin Square, by route of Eighth-street cars. Outward trips, through Green and Leverett Streets, Craigie's Bridge, and thence by inward route.

East Cambridge (Harvard-Square) Cars. — Inward trips, from Harvard Square, through Harvard Square, Cambridge, and Bridge Streets, and thence to Bowdoin Square, by route of the Eighth-street cars. Outward trips, through Green and Leverett Streets, Craigie's Bridge, and thence by inward route.

Union-Square (Somerville) Cars. — Inward trips, from Union Square (Somerville), through Milk Street (Somerville), Bridge Street (East Cambridge), and thence to Bowdoin Square, by route of the Eighth-street cars. Outward trips, through Green and Leverett Streets, Craigie's Bridge, and thence by inward route.

Somerville Cars. — Inward trips, from the company's stable at North Cambridge, through Elm and Milk Streets (Somerville), Bridge Street (East Cambridge), and thence to Bowdoin Square, by route of the Eighth-street cars. Outward trips, through Green and Leverett Streets, Craigie's Bridge, and thence by inward route.

THE

NEW ENGLAND ORGAN CO.

MANUFACTURE THE BEST

CABINET ORGAN

FOR THE HOME, CHURCH, OR CHAPEL.

Middlesex Railroad.

The cars of this line run to Charlestown, Somerville, Malden, Everett, and Winter Hill. The routes of the several lines are given below in detail.

Charlestown Neck Cars.—Inward trips, from Somerville line on Main Street (Charlestown), through Main Street, over Warren Bridge, through Beverly Street, Haymarket Square, and New Washington Street, to Temple Place. Outward trips, from Temple Place, through Tremont, Cornhill, Washington Streets, Haymarket Square, Charlestown Street, over Charles-river Bridge, through Charlestown Square, Warren, and Main Streets, to Somerville line.

Bunker-Hill Cars.—Inward trips, from station, near summit of Bunker-hill Street, through Bunker-hill, Vine, and Chelsea Streets, Charlestown Square, thence into Boston by same route as Neck cars. Outward trips, from Temple Place, same route as Neck cars, to Charlestown Square, thence through Warren, Henley, Chelsea, Vine, and Bunker-hill Streets, to the station.

Malden and Everett Cars.—Inward trips, from Malden Centre, through Main, Chelsea, School, and Charlestown Streets, over Malden Bridge, thence into Boston by same route as the Neck cars, to Haymarket Square, up Sudbury and Court, to Scollay Square. Outward trips, from Scollay Square, by route of the Neck cars, to the terminus of that line, thence to Malden Centre by the inward route.

Winter-Hill Cars.—Inward trips, from Winter Hill, in Somerville, through Broadway, to starting-point

---

SCOTCH SUITS
MADE TO ORDER AT
BRINE'S,
For $35.00.

---

365 WASHINGTON STREET. 365

of the Neck cars, thence into Boston by the Malden car route. Outward trips, from Scollay Square, by the Malden car route to the Somerville line, thence by Broadway (Somerville), to Winter Hill.

Union-Square Cars.—Inward trips from Union Square (Somerville), through Milk and Washington Streets, to Main Street (Charlestown), thence into Boston by route of the Malden cars. Outward trips from Scollay Square through Cornhill, Washington, Charlestown Streets, Charles-river Bridge, Main Street, to junction with inward route.

Lynn and Boston Railroad.

Chelsea Cars.—Inward trips, from Washington Avenue (Prattsville), Chelsea, through Washington Avenue, Broadway, Chelsea Bridge, Chelsea Street, Charlestown Square, Warren Bridge, Beverly, and Charlestown Streets, Haymarket Square, Sudbury and Court Streets, to Scollay Square. Outward trips, through Cornhill, New Washington, Haymarket Square, Charlestown Street, Charles-river Bridge, Charlestown Square, Park, Henley, and Chelsea Streets, Chelsea Bridge, Broadway, and Washington Avenue, to the station.

Revere Cars.—Inward trips, from Revere, over the Salem Turnpike, to Broadway in Chelsea, thence into Boston by route of the Chelsea cars. Outward trips, from Scollay Square, by the route of the Chelsea cars, to Broadway, thence by inward route of Revere cars to station.

Chelsea (Revere) Beach Cars.—From Revere Beach

COOLIDGE, SMITH, & CO.,
70 & 72 TREMONT STREET.

NEW STORE AND NEW GOODS.
Hosiery, Gloves, Straw Goods,
FLOWERS, RIBBONS, &c., &c.

to the Salem Turnpike, thence, by route of Revere cars, into Boston. Outward trips, from Scollay Square, by route of Revere cars, and inward route of Chelsea-beach cars, to the beach in Revere.

Lynn and Swampscott Cars. — Inward trips, from Lewis Street (Lynn), through Broad, Exchange, Central Square, Central Avenue, Oxford, Market, and South Common Streets, and Western Avenue, thence over Salem Turnpike, through Saugus and Revere, and by route of the Revere cars, into Boston. Outward trips, from Scollay Square, by route of Chelsea and Revere cars, and inward route of Lynn cars, to Lewis Street, Lynn.

Citizen's Omnibus Line.

From Charlestown to Boston, from foot of Salem Street (Charlestown), over Warren Bridge, through Causeway, Leverett, Green, Court, and Washington Streets, to Concord Street. From Boston to Charlestown, back over the same route.

Hack-Fares.

The following rates of fare have been established by the Board of Aldermen for all public hacks and carriages. Any driver who asks or receives more is subject to fine, and the forfeiture of license; and like penalties are inflicted for refusing to carry a passenger from any railroad-station or steamboat-landing to any part of the city.

Within the city proper, fifty cents for each pas-

A. STOWELL & CO.,

16 WINTER STREET,

IMPORTERS OF

CLOCKS, BRONZES, VASES,

TERRA COTTA AND LAVA GOODS.

Through Boston and Vicinity. 41

senger; but a driver may charge one dollar for carrying one person from points north of Cambridge, Court and State Streets, to points south of Dover, or west of Berkeley Streets. For more than one passenger, the charge is fifty cents each.

From one place to another in East Boston, from one place to another in South Boston, or from one place to another in Roxbury, the charge is fifty cents for each passenger.

Fares to Roxbury. For one passenger from a point north of Essex and Boylston Streets to any point in Roxbury, $2.50; the same for two persons; $3.00 for three persons; $3.00 for four persons.

For one passenger from points south of Essex and Boylston, but north of Dover and Berkeley, $2.00; the same amount for two persons; for three persons, $2.25; for four persons, $2.50. From points south of Dover and Berkeley Streets to any part of Roxbury, $1.25; for two persons, 75 cents each; for three or more persons, 50 cents each.

For one passenger between any part of the city proper and either South or East Boston, $1.00; for two or more persons, 75 cents each.

For one passenger from one point to another in Dorchester, $1.00; for each additional passenger, 50 cents. The rates of fare between Dorchester and the other parts of the city are complicated; but they will be found posted in every public carriage in the city.

Hackmen are not allowed to charge any thing extra for baggage carried. In Dorchester, however, they are allowed to charge 50 cents for each additional

---

THE

NEW ENGLAND ORGAN CO.

MANUFACTURE THE BEST

CABINET ORGAN

FOR THE HOME, CHURCH, OR CHAPEL.

trunk above two carried by one person. Children under four years of age are carried free; between four and twelve, half-rates only are allowed. Additional charges are permitted between midnight and six o'clock in the morning, according to definite rules, which every passenger may read for himself, as posted in the carriage.

Ferries to East Boston and Chelsea.

North Ferry. — From Lincoln's Wharf, foot of Battery Street, to foot of Border Street, East Boston.

South Ferry. — From foot of Eastern Avenue to foot of Lewis Street, East Boston.

Chelsea Ferry. — From foot of Hanover Street to Chelsea.

CONVEYANCES OUT OF BOSTON.
RAILROADS.

The railroads centering at Boston pass through nearly every village of Massachusetts within twenty miles of the city. The several railroads are briefly described below. The time-tables are changed so frequently that it would be useless to insert them in this book. They will at all times be found in the local papers.

Fitchburg Railroad.

From Boston to Fitchburg, fifty miles; double track for the whole distance. Connects at Fitchburg with the Vermont and Massachusetts Railroad to Montreal

---

SPRING AND FALL OVERCOATS,

AT ALL PRICES, AT

BRINE'S,

365   WASHINGTON STREET.   365

Station.	Miles.	Station.	Miles.
Medford Steps,	4½	Winter Hill,	2
Milk Row,	1½	Woburn Centre,	10
Mystic,	7½	Woburn W. S.,	10
North Woburn,	11½		

Boston and Maine Railroad.

Main line from Boston, station in Haymarket Square, to South Berwick Junction, seventy-four miles; is extending to Portland, Me., to which point it already connects by the P. S. and P. Railroad, and thence to all parts of Maine and Canada. Also connects to Manchester, Rochester, and the White Mountains. The principal places on its main line are Andover, Lawrence, Haverhill, and Dover, N.H. The following are all the stations on the main line and branches within twenty miles of Boston, alphabetically arranged, with the distance to each:—

Station.	Miles.	Station.	Miles.
Danvers Centre,	18	Reading,	12
Greenwood,	9	Somerville,	2
Lynnfield,	13	Stoneham,	8
Malden,	5	Wakefield,	10
Medford,	5	Wellington's,	3
Melrose,	7	West Danvers,	16
North Danvers,	19	Wilmington,	16
Park Street,	4	Wilmington Junction,	18
Putnamville,	20	Wyoming,	6

Boston and Providence Railroad.

From Boston to Providence, forty-four miles, double-track, with several branches. This road con-

THE
NEW ENGLAND ORGAN CO.

EMPLOY THE

MOST SKILFUL WORKMEN

IN PRODUCING THEIR

UNRIVALLED CABINET ORGANS.

nects at Mansfield for New Bedford. It also connects at Providence with the Shore Line to New York City and all points West and South. The principal places along the line and branches are Dedham, Pawtucket, Taunton, New Bedford, Attleboro', and Providence, R.I. The station in Boston is in Park Square, at the foot of the Common. The following are all the stations on this road and its branches within twenty miles of Boston, with the distance to each:—

Station.	Miles.	Station.	Miles.
Bird's,	17	Monterey,	6
Boylston,	3	Mount Hope,	5
Boylston Street,	3	Readville,	8½
Canton,	14	Roxbury,	2
Central,	6	Sharon,	17¼
Dedham,	9½	South Canton,	15
Forest Hills,	4	South Street,	5½
Green Lodge,	11	Spring Dale,	16
Highland,	7	Stoughton,	18
Hyde Park,	7	West Roxbury,	7
Jamaica Plain,	3½		

New York and New England Railroad.

The main division of this road extends from the station at the foot of Summer Street, Boston, to Putnam, Conn. Its Woonsocket Division enters Boston over the Albany Road, and passengers by that part of the line start from the station at the corner of Beach and Albany Streets. In the appended list of stations within twenty miles of Boston, those on the Woonsocket Division are marked with an asterisk (*).

NEW YORK CLOTHING.

CONSTANTLY ON HAND,

Garments from DEVLIN & CO., BROKAW BROS., CARHART, WHITFORD, & CO., and other celebrated New York houses.

ROBERT & GEORGE R. BRINE,
365 . . *WASHINGTON STREET.* . . 365

Through Boston and Vicinity. 47

Station.	Miles.	Station.	Miles.
Bird Street (Dorchester),	3	*Medfield,	19¼
Blue Hill,	9	Mount Bowdoin,	4
*Brookline,	4	*Needham,	12
*Chapel Station,	3	*Newton Centre,	8
*Charles River,	14½	*Newton Highlands,	9
*Chestnut Hill,	6½	* " Upper Falls,	10
Dorchester,	5	*Reservoir,	5¼
*Dover,	16	South Boston,	1
Ellis's,	13	Stoughton Street,	3
Everett's,	15	Tilton's,	18
*Highlandville,	11	Winslow's,	16
Hyde Park,	8	Walpole,	19
*Longwood,	3	West Walpole,	20
Mattapan,	6		

Boston and Albany Railroad.

From Boston to Albany, N.Y., two hundred and two miles, double track all the way, connecting at Albany with the New-York Central for all points West and South. Principal stations on the Boston and Albany Road, Worcester, Palmer, Springfield, and Pittsfield. Branches to Milford, North Adams, and Hudson, N.Y.; connects at Springfield with New Haven, Hartford, and Springfield Road for New York, and with Conn. River, R.R. for points northward. The station in Boston is at the corner of Beach and Albany Streets. The following is an alphabetical list of all stations within twenty miles of Boston on the Albany Road, with the distance in miles from Boston:—

Station.	Miles.	Station.	Miles.
Allston,	4	Longwood,	3
Auburndale,	10	Natick,	18

At 90 & 92 Tremont Street may be found a full line of Straw Goods at the very lowest prices.

WM. S. BUTLER & CO.

Station.	Miles.	Station.	Miles.
Brighton,	5	Newton,	7
Brookline,	4	" Lower Falls,	12
Chapel Station,	3	Newtonville,	8
Cottage Farm,	4	Rice's Crossing,	12
Faneuil,	6	Riverside,	11
Grantville,	13	Wellesley,	15
Lake Crossing,	12	West Newton,	9

Old Colony Railroad.

Main line from Boston to Newport, sixty-seven miles. Connects at Taunton with New Bedford and Taunton Railroad for New Bedford. This road has numerous branches, and is the Boston terminus of all the roads running along the south shore and to Cape Cod. The principal places reached by it are Taunton, New Bedford, Fall River, Newport and Plymouth. The ·Boston station is at the corner of Kneeland and South Streets. The following is a list of all stations on the main line and branches, with the distance of each, within twenty miles of Boston:

Station.	Miles.	Station.	Miles.
Abington,	19	North Abington,	18
Atlantic,	$5\frac{1}{2}$	North Bridgewater,	20
Braintree,	10	North Stoughton	17
Crescent Avenue,	2	Quincy,	8
East Milton,	$6\frac{1}{2}$	Quincy Adams,	$8\frac{1}{2}$
East Randolph,	15	Randolph,	15
East Stoughton,	17	Savin Hill,	3
Granite Bridge,	6	South Boston,	$\frac{1}{2}$
Harrison Square,	4	South Braintree,	11
Huntington Heights,	18	South Weymouth,	15
Mattapan,	8	Stoughton,	19
Milton Lower Mills,	7	West Quincy,	8
Neponset,	5	Wollaston Heights,	$6\frac{1}{2}$

A. STOWELL & Co.

IMPORTERS OF

Special Novelties in Fancy Jewelry,

GILT, JET, SHELL, OXYDIZED, ETC.

FANS! FANS! FANS!

16 WINTER STREET.

STEAMBOATS.
In the Harbor.

For Nahant. — Steamer Ulysses, from India Wharf, daily.

For Gloucester. — Steamer Sunshine, from north side of Central wharf, daily, at 1, P.M.

For Long Island, Lovell's Grove, Quincy Point, and Weymouth. — Steamer Massasoit, from Lewis Wharf, several times daily during the summer season.

For Hingham, Hull, and Nantasket Beach. — Steamers Rose Standish, John Romer, and John A. Andrew, from Rowe's Wharf, several times daily during the summer season.

For Gloucester and Magnolia. — Steamer Stamford, from Lewis Wharf, daily.

Outside.

For New York. — Metropolitan Line. Steamers Nereus, Neptune, and Gen. Whitney, from Central Wharf, Mondays, Wednesdays, and Saturdays, at 5, P.M.

For Philadelphia. — Steamers Saxon, and Norman, from Long Wharf, every Wednesday and Saturday, at 3, P.M.

THE NEW ENGLAND ORGAN CO.,
MANUFACTURERS OF
CABINET ORGANS.

OFFICE AND WAREROOMS, 1299 Washington St.,
MANUFACTORY, 49, 51, 53, 55, 57, & 59 Wareham St.,
BOSTON.

For Norfolk and Baltimore. — Steamers William Crane, William Lawrence, and George Appold, from Central Wharf, Tuesdays and Saturdays, at 2.30, P.M.

For Savannah. — Steamers Seminole and Oriental, from T Wharf, on the 10th, 20th, and 30th of each month.

For Portland. — Steamers John Brooks, and Forest City, from India Wharf, daily, at 7, P.M.

For Bath and the Kennebec River. — Steamer Star of the East, from Union Wharf, Tuesdays and Fridays, at 6, P.M.

For Bangor and the Penobscot River. — Steamers Cambridge and Katahdin, from Foster's Wharf, Mondays, Tuesdays, Thursdays, and Fridays, at 5.30, P.M.

For Eastport, Calais, and St. John, N.B. — Steamers New Brunswick and City of Portland, from Commercial Wharf, Mondays and Thursdays, at 8, A.M.

For Halifax and Prince Edward Island. — Steamer Carroll, from T Wharf, Saturdays, at 2, P.M.

For Liverpool. — Cunard Steamers China, Parthia, Atlas, Batavia, Marathon, and others, from Cunard Wharf, East Boston, Saturdays. Occasional trips on other days as advertised.

ALL THE LATEST STYLES OF
NECK WEAR
AT
BRINE'S,
365 Washington Street. 365

MEANS OF COMMUNICATION.
THE POST-OFFICE.

The Post-office is open daily, except Sundays, from 7.30, A.M., to 7.30, P.M., and is open all night to those hiring lock-boxes. The stamp-office is open until midnight. Hours of the money-order office from 10, A.M., to 5, P.M. There are two classes of receiving-boxes, for letters only, put up in various parts of the city; from those painted red, letters are collected hourly, from 8, A.M., until 7, P.M., and also at midnight. These boxes are put up at the corner of Pemberton Square and Tremont Street, on the Horticultural hall building, corner of Montgomery Place, and in Bowdoin Square, in the city proper; also at other horse-car stations. The black boxes are visited at 9, A.M., 12, M., 3, 6.30, and 9, P.M. All boxes are visited at 6 and 9, P.M., only on Sundays. Carriers deliver letters free in all parts of the city, if addressed to street and number, at 7.45 and 11.30, A.M., 2.30 4.15, and 5.30, P.M. Mails close at the main office, for principal points North and the Canadas, at 5 and 11, A.M., and 5. P.M.; for principal points East at 5, and 11, A.M., 2 and 7, P.M.; for the South and West, at 7½, A.M., 2 and 8, P.M.; for Albany and Western New York at 1, A.M., 2 and 4, P.M.; for the West at 1, A.M., 2 and 4 P.; for New-York City and the South at 7.30, 11, A.M., 2, and 8, P.M. Mails for all points in the immediate vicinity of Boston leave every hour between 7, A.M., and 7, P.M.

At 90 & 92 Tremont Street, may be found a full line of Straw Goods at the very lowest prices,

WM. S. BUTLER & CO.

TELEGRAPH OFFICES.

Western Union.

Principal Office, 109 State Street.

BRANCH OFFICES.

Post-Office.
Station A, Post-Office, So. End.
Boston Highlands (P. Office).
218 Devonshire St.
Shoe and Leather Exchange.
127 Federal Street.
Old State House.
St. James Hotel.
American House.
Parker House.
Revere House.
Metropolitan Hotel.

Tremont House.
United States Hotel.
Clarendon Hotel.
Boston & Maine Station.
Boston & Albany Station.
Boston & Providence Station.
Old Colony Station.
Boston & Fitchburg Station.
Boston and Lowell Station.
Eastern Station.
N.Y. & N.E. R.R. Station
Commercial Wharf.

Franklin Telegraph.

Principal Office, 112 State Street.

BRANCH OFFICES.

31 State Street.
615 Washington Street.
110 High Street.

90 Franklin Street.
114 Commercial Wharf.
200 Congress Street.

EXPRESSES.

Nearly all expresses are concentrated in Court Square, and at No. 3 Washington Street. The location of the great general express companies is as follow: —

A. STOWELL & CO.,
BOSTON.
ROMAN GOLD NECKLACES,
Lockets, Pendants, and Crosses,
14Kt. WATCH CHAINS AND GENTLEMEN'S SEALS.
16 Winter Street.

Adams. — Nos. 28 to 40, Court Street.
Eastern. — No. 103, Devonshire Street.
United States and Canada. — Nos. 39 and 40, Court Square.
Wells, Fargo, & Co. — No. 96, Washington Street.

PLACES OF INTEREST.
PUBLIC BUILDINGS.

The following public buildings in and about Boston may be visited and examined. Where nothing to the contrary is stated, they may be visited at any hour and on any day, except Sunday.

City Hall. — On School Street.

State House. — Beacon Street. The cupola may be visited any day, except during the session of the Legislature. The rotunda and offices are open at all times during the daytime.

County Court House. — Court Square.

Suffolk-County Jail. — Charles Street, near Cambridge Street.

Faneuil Hall. — Always open. Entrance at east end of the hall.

Faneuil-Hall (Quincy) Market. — Between North and South Market Streets. Open during every day.

Public Library. — Boylston Street, near Tremont. Open to all, from 9, A.M., during every day and evening, except Sundays.

Boston Athenæum. — Beacon Street, near Somerset Street. Open every day from 9, A.M., until 6,

---

THE
NEW ENGLAND ORGAN CO.
MANUFACTURE THE BEST

CABINET ORGAN
FOR THE HOME, CHURCH, OR CHAPEL

P.M. This is a private library, but visitors are admitted.

Boston Athenœum Gallery. — In Athenæum Building, as above. Open during every day, except Sundays, on payment of a small fee.

Old State House. — Head of State Street. This is not now a public building, but it possesses a great deal of historic interest. It may be visited at any time.

City Hospital. — Harrison Avenue, opposite Worcester Square. Admittance only by permit.

Massachusetts General Hospital. — Blossom Street. Admittance only by permit.

Beacon-Hill Reservoir. — In the Square bounded by Hancock, Derne, Temple, and Mount Vernon Streets. A solid granite structure worthy to be examined.

Custom House. — State Street. Admission during business hours.

Post Office. — Devonshire, Milk, & Water Streets & Post-office Square. Admission during any hour of the day or night.

United States Court House. — Corner of Tremont Street and Temple Place.

Almshouse. — South Boston.
House of Correction. — South Boston.
House of Industry. — South Boston.
House of Refuge. — South Boston.
Insane Hospital. — South Boston.
Perkins Institute for the Blind. — Broadway, South Boston. Admission by permit, to be obtained on application at No. 20 Bromfield Street.

Boston Society of Natural History. — Corner of

WHITE MARSEILLES AND DUCK VESTS,

$1, $1.50, $2, at

BRINE'S,

365 Washington Street. 365

Through Boston and Vicinity. 55

Berkeley and Boylston Streets. Admission to all on Wednesdays and Saturdays, between the hours of 10, A.M., and 2, P.M.
Institute of Technology. — Boylston Street, between Berkeley and Clarendon.
Masonic Temple. — Corner of Boylston and Tremont Streets.
New Odd Fellows' Hall. — Corner of Berkeley and Tremont Streets.
Horticultural Hall. — Corner of Tremont and Bromfield Streets.
New Post Office. — Corner of Water and Devonshire Streets.
Charitable Mechanics' Association Building. — Corner of Bedford and Chauncy Streets.
Historic Genealogical Society. — 17 Somerset Street.
Washington Market. — Corner of Washington and Lenox Streets.
Museum of Fine Arts. — Huntington Avenue (in process of erection).

Statues and Monuments.

Many of the following are mentioned elsewhere in this Guide Book. No monuments to be found in any of the burying-grounds are included in this list.
Soldiers' Monument. — Foundation laid on Flagstaff Hill, on the Common.
Statue of Everett. — Public Garden, Beacon-street side.
Equestrian Statue of Washington. — Public Garden, Arlington-street entrance.

JAPANESE FANS,

Silk Fans, Autograph Fans, Feather Fans,

OF ALL KINDS AND PRICES, AT

WILLIAM S. BUTLER & CO.'S,

90 & 92 TREMONT STREET.

Venus rising from the Sea. — Public Garden, near Arlington-street entrance.
Ether Monument. — Public Garden, north-west part.
Statue of Franklin. — In front of City Hall.
Statue of Andrew. — Doric Hall, State House.
Statue of Washington. — Doric Hall, State House.
Statue of Mann. — In front of State House.
Statue of Webster. — In front of State House.
Statue of Hamilton. — Commonwealth Avenue, near Arlington Street.
Statue of Aristides. — Louisburg Square.
Statue of Columbus. — Louisburg Square.
Statue of Beethoven. — Music Hall.
Bunker-Hill Monument. — Bunker-hill Square, Charlestown.
Chelsea Soldiers' Monument. — Chelsea Common.
Cambridge Soldiers' Monument. — Cambridge Common.

Parks and Squares.

The following are the principal parks and open spaces in Boston, and their location.

The Common. — Bounded by Tremont, Boylston, Charles, Beacon, and Park Streets.

The Public Garden. — Bounded by Boylston, Arlington, Beacon, and Charles Streets.

Commonwealth Avenue. — From Arlington Street westward.

Louisburg Square. — Bounded by Mount Vernon, West Cedar, and Pinckney Streets.

Haymarket Square. — At the junction of Washington, Charlestown, and Merrimac Streets.

MOURNING JEWELRY,
ONYX AND WHITBY JET.
CHOICE DESIGNS IN EACH.
NECKLACES, BROOCHES, EARRINGS, CROSSES, AND PENDANTS,
MOUNTED WITH OR WITHOUT GOLD.
With Pearls, and Plain.

Dock Square.— Washington, Exchange, and Cornhill.
Post Office Square. — Water, Congress, and Milk Streets.
Union Park. — From 93 Shawmut Avenue to Tremont Street.
Blackstone Square. — Bounded by West Brookline, Washington, and West Newton Streets, and Shawmut Avenue.
Franklin Square. — Bounded by East Brookline, Washington, East-Newton, and James Streets.
Rutland Square. — From 703 Tremont Street to Columbus Avenue.
Concord Square. — From 725 Tremont Street to Columbus Avenue.
Worcester Square. — From 1678 Washington Street to 799 Harrison Avenue.
Chester Square. — From 1755 Washington Street to 772 Tremont Street.
Chester Park. — From 1756 Washington Street to 773 Albany Street.
West Chester Park. — From 781 Tremont Street to Columbus Avenue.
Eliot Square. — Junction of Roxbury, Dudley, and Centre Streets, Roxbury.
Eyleston Square. — From 3076 Washington, to 387 Walnut Avenue, Roxbury.
Maverick Square. — Bounded by Lewis, Maverick, Meridian, Chelsea, and Sumner Streets, East Boston.
Central Square. — Junction of Border, Liverpool, Meridian, Bennington, and Saratoga Streets, East Boston.

THE NEW ENGLAND ORGAN CO.,

MANUFACTURERS OF

CABINET ORGANS.

OFFICE AND WAREROOMS, 1299 Washington St.,

MANUFACTORY, 49, 51, 53, 55, 57, & 59 Wareham St.,

BOSTON.

Independence Square. — Bounded by M, Second, and N Streets, and Broadway, South Boston.

The Principal Wharves.

Boston is surrounded with wharves, from Warren Bridge, on Charles River, to Federal-street Bridge, across Fort Point Channel. There are also important wharves in South Boston, and some of the most extensive in the harbor at East Boston. Upon most of these are long lines of substantial warehouses. In this place we can but mention a few of the more important wharves, as follows, beginning at the northern part of the city and proceeding southward: —

Constitution. — From 411 Commercial Street.
Lincoln. — From 365 Commercial Street.
Union. — From 323 Commercial Street.
Sargent's. — From 293 Commercial Street, foot of Fleet Street.
Lewis. — From 40 Atlantic Avenue.
Commercial. — From 90 Atlantic Avenue.
T. — From 46 Long Wharf.
Long. — Foot of State Street.
Central. — 244 Atlantic Avenue.
India. — 304 Atlantic Avenue.
Rowe's. — From 144 Broad Street.
Liverpool. — Atlantic Avenue.
Russia. — 550 Atlantic Avenue.
Boston. — From First Street, South Boston.
Ferry. — Foot of Lewis Street, East Boston.
Eastern Railroad. — From Marginal, opposite Orleans Street, East Boston.

HOME-SPUN SUITS,

READY-MADE,

—AT—

BRINE'S,

365   Washington Street.   365

Cunard. — From Marginal, opposite Orleans Street, East Boston.
Grand-Junction Wharves. — From Marginal Street, East Boston

Markets.

Faneuil Hall. — Faneuil-hall building and Quincy building, between North and South Market Streets.
Blackstone. — From 72 to 92 Blackstone Street.
Lakeman. — Corner of Blackstone and North Streets.
Union. — Washington, near Haymarket Square.
Central. — No. 50 North Street.
Merrimac. — Corner of Merrimac and Market Streets.
Suffolk. — Corner of Portland and Sudbury Streets.
Boylston. — Corner of Washington and Boylston Streets.
St. Charles. — Corner of Beach and Lincoln Streets.
Williams. — Corner of Washington and East-Dover Streets.
Washington. — Corner of Washington and Lenox Streets.
Tremont. — No. 923 Tremont Street.
Franklin. — 108 Beach Street.

Libraries.

American Academy of Arts and Sciences, Athenæum Building, Beacon Street.
American Baptist Missionary Union, Tremont Temple, room 2.
Boston Athenæum, Athenæum Building, Beacon Street.

JAPANESE FANS,

Silk Fans, Autograph Fans, Feather Fans,

OF ALL KINDS AND PRICES, AT

WILLIAM S. BUTLER & CO.'S,

90 & 92 TREMONT STREET.

Boston Deaf Mute Library and Mission, Washington Street, room 7.
Boston Library Society, No. 18 Boylston Place.
Boston Public Library, Boylston Street, near Tremont. Open to all.
Boston Society of Natural History, Berkeley Street, between Newbury and Boylston.
Boston University, 36 Bromfield Street.
Boston Young Men's Christian Association, corner of Eliot and Tremont Streets.
Boston Young Men's Christian Union, No. 520 Washington Street.
Charlestown Library, Charlestown.
Clarendon Library, No. 87 Clarendon Street.
Congregational Library, Beacon, corner Somerset Street.
Dorchester Athenæum, corner Pleasant and Cottage Streets (D.).
East Boston Branch Public Library, Meridian, corner Paris Streets.
Franklin Typographical Society, No. 186 Washington Street.
General Theological Library, No. 12 West Street.
Holton Branch City Library, Rockland Street, Brighton.
Law Library, No. 14 Court House, Court Square.
Massachusetts Historical Society, Tremont Street, between Pemberton Square and Beacon Street.
Massachusetts Horticultural Society, corner Tremont and Bromfield Streets.
Mattapan Library, corner Park and Exchange Streets (D.).
Mechanic Apprentices' Library Association, No. 43 Chauncy Street.
Mercantile Library Association, No. 1371 Washington Street.
New Church Free Library, No. 2 Hamilton Place.
New England Historical Genealogical Society, Somerset Street, near Allston.
Roxbury Athenæum, No. 27 Guild Row (R.).
South Boston Branch Public Library, 372 West Broadway.
West Roxbury Free Library, Centre, near Mount Vernon Street (Ward 17).

A. STOWELL & CO.,

16 WINTER STREET,

IMPORTERS OF

CLOCKS, BRONZES, VASES,

TERRA COTTA AND LAVA GOODS.

Daily Newspapers.

Boston Daily Advertiser (morning), No. 29 Court Street.
Boston Post (morning), Milk Street.
Boston Daily Globe (morning), 238 Washington Street.
Boston Daily Journal (morning and evening), 264 Washington Street.
Boston Herald (morning and evening), 241 Washington Street.
Boston Daily News (evening), 300 Washington Street.
Boston Transcript (evening), 324 Washington Street.
Boston Traveller (evening), No. 31, State Street.

Prominent Churches.

First Church (Cong. Un.), Marlboro', c. Berkeley, Rufus Ellis.
King's Chapel (Cong. Un.), Tremont, corner School, Henry W. Foote.
South Congregational (Cong. Un.), Union-Park St., Edward E. Hale.
Church of the Disciples (Cong. Un.), W. Brookline St., J. F. Clarke.
West Boston Society (Cong. Un.), Lynde St., Cyrus A. Bartol.
Old South Church (Cong. Trin.), Dartmouth, cor. of Boylston, Jacob M. Manning.
Park-street Church (Cong. Trin.), Tremont, corner Park.
Central Church (Cong. Trin.), Berkeley, corner Newbury, J. DeWitt.
Shawmut Church (Cong. Trin.), Tremont, cor. Brookline, E. B. Webb.
Christ Church (Epis.) Salem Street, Henry Burroughs, jun.
Trinity Church (Epis.), Services at Institute of Technology, Phillips Brooks.
Church of the Advent (Epis.), Bowdoin St., Samuel Cutter.
Emanuel Church (Epis.), Newbury Street, A. H. Vinton.
Tremont-street Methodist Episcopal, Tremont St., J. E. Cookman.
First Baptist Ch., Somerset St., R. H. Neale & J. T. Beckley.
Clarendon-street Ch. (Bapt.), Clarendon, corner Montgom'y, A. J. Gordon.

THE

NEW ENGLAND ORGAN CO.

EMPLOY THE

MOST SKILFUL WORKMEN

IN PRODUCING THEIR

UNRIVALLED CABINET ORGANS.

Union-Temple Ch. (Bapt.), Tremont Temple, Geo. C. Lorimer.
Shawmut-avenue Ch. (Bapt.), Shawmut Ave., Wayland Hoyt.
Second Universalist, Columbus Ave., corner Clarendon, A. A. Miner.
East Boston Universalist, Central Square, Seldon Gilbert.
New Jerusalem Ch. (Sweden'n), Bowdoin St., James Reed.
Cathedral Chapel of Holy Cross (Rom. Cath.), Castle St.
Church of the Holy Trinity (Rom. Cath.), Suffolk Street.
Church of the Immaculate Conception (Rom. Cath.), Harrison Ave.

Places of Amusement.

Theatres.

Boston Theatre. — The largest theatre in Boston. It is conducted on the "star" system. There is a very good stock company, and the theatre always has some fresh attractions, — a great star actor, a spectacular drama, or German, Italian, or English opera. It is situated on Washington Street, near West. Thayer and Tompkins, proprietors; L. R. Shewell, manager.

Globe Theatre. — One of the most beautiful and completely-furnished theatres in the country. It is conducted partly on the stock company and partly on the star principle. It is on Washington Street, near Essex. Arthur Cheney proprietor.

Boston Museum. — This is the favorite orthodox theatre of Boston, and is situated on Tremont Street, near Court. It is the home of comedy in Boston, and generally discards the star system. It is with this theatre that the famous comedian, William Warren, has been connected so long. The company is excellent. R. M. Field, manager.

BARGAINS IN SUMMER GOODS.

LINEN ULSTERS,

MOHAIR ULSTERS,

ALPACA COATS,

AT

BRINE'S,

365 WASHINGTON STREET. 365

Howard Athenæum. — Situated on Howard Street. This was once a theatre for the legitimate drama. It is now wholly given up to variety entertainments, and is nightly crowded with the lovers of that class of amusement. The attractions, which are of every variety, succeed each other with bewildering rapidity.

Boylston Museum. — Washington, near Boylston Street. Many curiosities, natural and otherwise are exhibited here, and dramatic performances are given daily.

Music and Lecture Halls.

The following are some of the more important of the halls used for public concerts, lectures, and similar entertainments.

Music Hall. — No. 15 Winter Street. This is the largest hall in Boston. It is constantly in use for concerts, lectures, fairs, and other entertainments. Admission can be obtained at any time during the day, on the payment of a fee. The hall is well worthy of a visit by all who have not entered it.

Bumstead Hall. — This is a small hall beneath the grand Music Hall, and is often used in connection with the latter. It is also the head-quarters of the Handel and Haydn Society, and the place for its rehearsals.

Horticultural Hall. — There are two fine halls in the Horticultural Building, corner of Tremont and Bromfield Streets. They are used for chamber concerts, fairs, parties, dances, lectures, and religious discourses on certain Sunday afternoons.

DON'T FORGET

to visit the NEW STORE of

COOLIDGE, SMITH, & CO.,

70 & 72 Tremont Street,

for all kinds of

MILLINERY GOODS.

Faneuil Hall. — In Faneuil-hall Square. This historic hall is open to visitors throughout the day. It is used only for public meetings; and the use of it is granted by the city government, if at all, without fee.

Wesleyan Association Hall. — Bromfield Street, opposite Province. This is a small but very pleasant hall, often used for concerts, for lectures, and for meetings of associations.

Tremont Temple. — Tremont Street, near School. This is a very large and fine hall, used for religious exercises on Sunday, and very frequently during the week for conventions, lectures, readings, and concerts. It was in this hall that Charles Dickens gave his readings on his last visit to America.

Meionaon. — A small hall under Tremont Temple.

Parker Memorial Hall. — This hall at the corner of Berkeley and Appleton Streets, was erected by the society founded by the late Theodore Parker. It is used for religious services, concerts, lectures, &c.

Paine Memorial Hall, on Appleton, near Berkeley Street, was erected by the admirers of Thomas Paine, and is used for religious services, lectures, concerts, fairs, &c.

Beethoven Hall. — Washington Street, nearly opposite the Globe Theatre. A fine new hall, specially adapted for musical and miscellaneous entertainments.

Institute Hall. — No. 113 Dudley Street, Roxbury. The largest and finest Hall at the Highlands, and used for all purposes to which a public hall is devoted.

A. STOWELL & CO.,

16 Winter Street,

Importers of Fine French Marble Clocks,

CHOICE BRONZE,

VIENNA FANCY GOODS.

John A. Andrew Hall. — Corner of Chauncy and Eessex Streets. A small hall used for various purposes.

Lowell Institute. — Rear of 223 Washington Street. This hall is the place where most of the Lowell Institute free lectures are delivered.

THE CITY GOVERNMENT FOR 1872.

Mayor. — Samuel C. Cobb.
Chairman Board of Aldermen. — John T. Clark.
President Common Council. — H. J. Boardman.
City Clerk. — S. F. McCleary.
Clerk of Committees. — James M. Bugbee.
City Solicitor. — John P. Healy.
City Treasurer. — Frederick U. Tracy.*
Auditor. — Alfred T. Turner.
City Physician. — Samuel A. Green, M.D.
Port Physician. — C. Irving Fisher.
Superintendent of Streets. — Charles Harris.
Superintendent of Health. — G. W. Forrestall.
President Water Board. — John A. Haven.
Chairman Overseers of Poor. — Frederick W. Lincoln.
President Board of Directors for Public Institutions. — J. Putnam Bradlee.
Street Commissioners. — Newton Talbot, Joseph Smith, Isaac S. Burrill.

* Deceased.

THE NEW ENGLAND
CABINET ORGAN.

THE FAVORITE INSTRUMENT FOR THE HOME CIRCLE.

Illustrated Catalogue sent on application.

POLICE DEPARTMENT.

Chief of Police. — Edward H. Savage.
Deputy Chief. — James Quinn.

Police Stations.

1. No. 209 Hanover, near Cross Street.
2. No. 21 Court Square, corner Williams Court.
3. Joy Street, near Cambridge.
4. No. 23 La Grange Street.
5. East-Dedham Street.
6. Broadway, near C Street (South Boston).
7. Paris Street (East Boston).
8. Corner Commercial and Salutation Streets.
9. Dudley, corner Mt. Pleasant Avenue.
10. Junction Washington and Tremont Streets.
11. Hancock Street (Dorchester).
12. Fourth Street, near K.
13. Seavems Avenue (Jamaica Plain).
14. Washington Street (Brighton Centre).
15. Harvard Street, corner City Square (Charlestown).

FIRE DEPARTMENT.

The headquarters of the Fire Department are at City Hall. The fire commissioners (nominated by the Mayor and confirmed by the Council) are Alfred P. Rockwell, David Chamberlain, and Timothy T. Sawyer; Chief Engineer, Wm. A. Green; with ten assistant engineers and two call engineers, appointed by the Commissioners. The fire department has been lately re-organized, and is now one of the most efficient in the country. Uniformed patrolmen are

BLACK FROCKS,
BLACK PANTALOONS,
BLACK VESTS.

FULL ASSORTMENT AT

BRINE'S,
365   Washington Street.   365

constantly on duty, and the officers and men at the engine houses, are ready, day and night, to respond to the alarms of fire. There are twenty-nine steam fire engines, located, besides five held in reserve, each officered by a foreman, assistant foreman, engine man, assistant engine man, and eight hosemen. The city proper has but about a quarter of this number of engines, the rest being distributed in South and East Boston, and the newly annexed wards. There are eleven hook and ladder companies, and fifteen horse hose companies, all thoroughly officered. There are also seven chemical engines, which are often of great assistance in extinguishing fires, being lighter and more readily set to work than the steamers. There is also a fire-boat for use around the water front. The whole force employed in the Fire Department is seven hundred men.

FIRE ALARMS.

The Fire Alarm Telegraph is under charge of Supt. John F. Kennard, whose headquarters are at City Hall. From the dome of the City Hall radiate all the wires which, connected with the bells in churches and other public edifices, and the gongs in engine houses, sound the alarm simultaneously in all sections of the city, giving the district in which the fire occurs, the number having been previously telegraphed from the locality to City Hall. The system is thus explained: to announce the existence of a fire near Box No. 41 (Old South Church), the bells will strike *four*, make a pause of a few seconds, then strike *one*,

WM. S. BUTLER & CO.,

IMPORTERS AND RETAILERS OF

MILLINERY GOODS, HOSIERY, GLOVES, SMALL WARES, &c.,

90 TREMONT STREET, BOSTON. 92

NEXT DOOR TO METROPOLITAN R.R. OFFICE.

thus: 4 — 1. This will be repeated at intervals of about one minute. For a fire near Box No. 145 (South Boston Point) the bells will strike *one*, make a pause, then strike *four*, another pause, then strike *five*, thus, 1 — 4 — 5.

33, followed by box number, indicates fire in West-Roxbury district. 44, followed by box number, indicates fire in Charlestown district. 55 indicates fire in Brighton district, where the local alarm is given by the ringing of bells.

Second alarms are sounded by striking ten blows. Third alarms are sounded by striking twelve blows twice, thus: 12 — 12.

In cases where the entire department is required, alarms are sounded by striking twelve blows three times, thus: 12 — 12 — 12.

In cases where hook-and-ladder companies *only* are wanted, signal to be given by striking ten blows once, with the number of the company struck twice, thus: Hook and Ladder No. 1, 10—1—1. Hook and Ladder No. 4, 10—4—4. Hook and Ladder No. 7, 10—7—7.

If more than one hook-and-ladder company is wanted, the signal will be given thus: Hook and Ladder 1 and 3, 10—1—1—3—3. Hook and Ladder, 2 and 4, 10—2—2—4—4. Hook and Ladder 5 and 7, 10—5—5—7—7. The following shows the location of all the alarm-boxes in the city: —

A. STOWELL & CO.,

16 WINTER STREET,

IMPORTERS OF

TORTOISE-SHELL COMBS.

IMITATION SHELL COMBS IN GREAT VARIETY.

SPECIAL STYLES OF OUR OWN SUGGESTION.

Numbers and Localities of the Boxes.

2. Cor Charter st & Phipps pl
3. Cor Hull & Snowhill sts
4. B & M Freight Depot
5. Cor Causeway & Lowell
6. Cor Leverett & Willard
7. Cor Poplar & Spring sts
8. Merrimac House, Merrimac st
9. Constitution Wharf
12. Cor Cooper & Endicott
13. Richmond near Hanover
14. Cor Com st & Eastern av
15. Cor Comer'l & Richmond
16. East end of Faneuil Hall
17. Cor. Hanover & Salem sts
18. Quincy House
19. Boston & Maine Depot
21. Cor Sudbury & Hawkins
23. Cambridge, op Bowdoin
24. North Russell st (Church)
25. West City Stables
26. West Cedar, n. Cambridge
27. River st (Engine House 10)
28. Spruce st, Club House
29. Beacon & Clarendon sts
31. Cor Beacon & Beaver sts
32. Cor Pinckney & Anderson
34. Cor Hancock & Myrtle
35. Beacon st, cor Somerset
36. Court sq (Police Sta No. 2)
37. Cor India st & Central whf
38. Cor Atlantic av & Long wh
39. Mason st, Engine Ho 26
41. Cor Washington & Milk
42. Cor Winter & Central pl
43. Cor Bedf'd st & Suffolk pl
45. Cor Federal & Franklin
46. Cor Milk & Oliver sts
47. Broad st, op Rowe's whf
48. N Y & N E R R Station
49. Summer, op Hawley st
51. Cor Purchase & Pearl
52. Cor Bedford & Lincoln sts
53. Cor Wash'ton & Boylston
54. Cor Beach & Hudson sts
56. Old Colony Depot
57. Hudson st (Hose House 2)
58. B. & A. Freight Depot
59. East st (School House)
61. Warrenton, near Tremont
62. Cor Pleasant & Eliot sts
63. Berkeley, near Com'lth av
64. Cor Wash st & Indiana pl
65. Cor Har ave & Seneca st
67. Cor Wash'ton & Common
68. Cor Har'n av & Wareham
69. Cor Dover & Albany sts
71. Cor Warren av & Berkeley
72. Washington, near Dover
73. Cor Shawmut av & Wal'm
74. Dedham st (Police Sta 5)
75. Shawmut av (H House 5)
76. Cor Tremont & Rutland sq
78. South City Stables
79. Cor Beacon & Exeter sts
81. Cor W Canton & Appleton
82. North'ton (Eng House 23)
83. Cor Tremont & Camden
84. Parker (Engine House 22)
85. Cor Castle & Albion sts
86. Commonwealth Hotel
87. Cor Columbus av & Buckingham st
119. Gasometer, near Federal street Bridge

THE

NEW ENGLAND ORGAN CO.

EMPLOY THE

MOST SKILFUL WORKMEN

IN PRODUCING THEIR

UNRIVALLED CABINET ORGANS.

South Boston.

121. Cor First & A sts
123. Cor Broadway & Dor av
124. Broadway (Police Sta 6)
125. Cor Dorchester av & Dorr
126. Cor Broadway & E street
127. Cor Eighth & E sts
128. Cor Dorch'r av & Dor'r st
129. Cor Sixth & B sts
131. Cor Eighth & G sts
132. Cor Broadway & Dorch'r
134. Cor Fifth & D st
135. Cor Eighth & K sts
136. Cor First & K sts
137. Fourth st, between K & L
138. House of Correction (gate)
141. Boston Wharf
142. Page's Mill, First st
143. Cor Dorchester & Seventh
145. Cor Fourth & O sts
146. American Steam Safe Works, City Point
147. Storey, near G st
148. N. Y. & N. E. R. R. Repair Shop

East Boston.

151. Ferry House (South)
152. Cor Sumner and Lamson
153. Cor Webster & Orleans
154. Cor Maverick & Meridian
156. Cor Sumner & Border sts
157. Cor Decatur & Liverpool
158. Cor Paris & Decatur sts
161. Grand Junction Yard
162. Cor Bennington st & Central sq
163. Cor Chelsea & Marion sts
164. Simpson's whf, Marginal
165. Cor Marion & Trenton
167. Forge Works, Maverick st
171. Porter's whf, Border st
172. Pottery Works, 146 Condor
173. Cor Eagle & Glendon sts
174. Cor Brooks & Saratoga
175. Cor Chelsea & Saratoga sts
176. Sanborn Tube Works, Saratoga st
178. Cor Moore & Saratoga sts
182. Cor Sumner & Paris sts
183. Cor Cottage & Everett sts
184. Cor Meridian & Princeton
185. Cor Putnam & Lexington

Roxbury District.

212. Cor Albany & Hampden
213. Cor Norfolk av & Hampden sts
214. Cor Washington & Arnold
215. Cor Tremont & Cabot sts
216. Cor Ruggles & Parker sts
217. Cor Ruggles & Tremont
218. Junc Wash'n & Warren

D. B. DIAGONAL FROCKS AND VESTS,

—AT—

BRINE'S,

365   WASHINGTON STREET.   365

219. Longwood av (Carpet Factory)
231. Eustis, near Washington
232. Cor Eustis & Dearborn sts
234. Police Station 9, Dudley
235. Cor Winslow & Dudley sts
236. Cor Cabot & Culvert
237. Dudley st, Gas Co's Office
239. Swett st, n Old Hospital
239. Shawmut av, Horse R. R. Stable
241. Cor Warren st & Waln't av
242. Cor Clifford st & Blue-hill av
243. Engine House 14, Centre
245. Police Station 10, Pynchon
246. Longwood (Chemical Engine House, No. 3)
247. Cor Tremont & Francis sts
248. Repair Shop, B. & P. R.R.
249. Burkhardt's Brewery, Parker st
251. Cor Highland & Cedar sts
252. Cor Dale st & Shawmut av
253. Cor Warren st & Blue-hill av
254. Cor Pynchon & Heath sts
256. School House, Heath st
257. Cor Warren & Quincy sts
258. Cor Tremont & Downer
261. Shawmut av, n Egleston sq
262. Cor Highland & Marcella
263. Cor Center & Creighton
264. Cor Walnut av. & Munroe

Dorchester District.

312. Cor Boston & Mt. Vernon
313. Cor Dorch'r av & Cottage
314. Engine House 21, Boston
315. Cor Stoughton & Cottage
316. Engine House 17, Meeting House Hill
317. Cor Bird & Ceylon sts
318. Stoughton-st Station (N. Y. & N. E. R. R.)
319. Norfolk av, n R. R. Bridge
321. Savin Hill
323. Glover's corner
324. Cor Green & Bowdoin sts
325. Field's corner
326. Harrison square
327. Adams st, op Neponset av
328. Putnam's Nail Works (Port Norfolk)
341. Cor Commercial & Preston
342. Cor Neponset av and Minot st
343. Cor Water & Walnut sts
345. Cor Adams & Granite sts
346. Cor Dorchester av & Codman sts
347. Cor Wash st & Warren pl
348. Cor Richmond & Adams
351. Cor Wash st & Dorch'r av
352. Engine House 16, Temple
353. Engine House 19, Norfolk
354. Cor Norfolk & Madison sts
356. Cor Washing'n & Norfolk
357. Engine House 18, Harv'rd
361. Cor. Harvard st & Blue-hill av
362. Mt. Hope Cemetery (Superintendent's House.)

WM. S. BUTLER & CO.,

IMPORTERS AND RETAILERS OF

MILLINERY GOODS, HOSIERY, GLOVES, SMALL WARES, &c.,

90 TREMONT STREET, BOSTON. 92

NEXT DOOR TO METROPOLITAN R.R. OFFICE.

Former Numbering Unchanged.

Charlestown District.

3. Holmes' Factory, Medford
4. 305 Medford street
5. Cor Medford & Bunker-Hill sts
6. Cor Gardiner & Main sts
7. Cor Main & Eden sts
8. Main, foot of Baldwin sts
9. Cor Cambridge & Bright'n
12. Cor School & Main sts
13. Cor Wash'ton & Union sts
14. Front, foot of Arrow st
15. Fitchburg Railroad Yard
16. Cor Harvard & Main sts
17. Cor Chapman & Richm'd
21. Cor City sq & Chambers
23. Cor Henley st & Henley pl
24. Cor Tufts, Bunker-Hill & Vine sts
25. Cor Concord & Bunker Hill sts
26. Wallace Court
31. Cor Bunker Hill & Webster
32. Cor Walker & Russell sts
34. 21 Medford st
35. Medford st (Waterman's Mill)
41. Engine House 27 Elm st
42. Navy Yard

West Roxbury District.

4. Engine House 28, Centre
5. Cor Pond & Prince sts
6. Cor Prince & Perkins sts
7. Cor May & Centre sts
13. Jamaica Plain R. R. Station
14. Boylston-st R. R. Station
15. Hyde's Corner
16. Forest Hills R. R. Station
23. Cor South & Key sts
24. Roslindale R. R. Station
25. Central R. R. Station
32. W. Roxbury R. R. Station
34. Cor School st & Shawmut
42. Mt. Hope R. R. Station
43. Canterbury School House
51. Cor Scarboro' & Walnut

PUBLIC BATHING PLACES.

The public baths are open June 1st, and are kept open daily until September 30th each year, and are free to all. Those marked with an asterisk (*) are

---

A. STOWELL & CO.,

16 Winter Street,

Importers of Fine French Marble Clocks,

CHOICE BRONZE,

VIENNA FANCY GOODS.

for women and girls. All the others are for men and boys.

1. West-Boston Bridge, foot of Cambridge.
2. Charles-river Bridge, near Causeway.
*3. Warren Bridge.
4. East Boston, Sectional Dock, Border Street.
*5. East Boston, Sectional Dock, 96 Border Street.
6. Federal-street Bridge.
7. Mount-Washington-avenue Bridge.
*8. South Boston, foot of L Street.
9. South Boston, foot of Fifth Street.
10. Dover-street Bridge, South Pier.
*11. Dover-street Bridge, South Pier.
12. Cabot Street, Highlands.
*13. Cabot Street, Highlands.
14. Norfolk Avenue.
15. Commercial Point, Dorchester.
16. Maverick Street, East Boston.
17. Chelsea Bridge, Charlestown.
*18. Chelsea Bridge, Charlestown.
19. Malden Bridge, Charlestown.

HOTELS AND RESTAURANTS.

Hotels.

The following partial list of the hotels in Boston may be of use to strangers stopping in the city. The houses are classified. Those which are wholly or chiefly boarding or family hotels are marked with an asterisk (*). Those which are large and first-class in every respect are printed in SMALL CAPITALS, and those which are smaller in size, though perhaps equally worthy of patronage, are printed in *italics*.

I consider the Cabinet Organs manufactured by the

NEW ENGLAND ORGAN COMPANY

fully equal in tone, mechanism, and appearance to those produced in any establishment in the country; and would call attention to the "soft register," or Dulciana, as being uncommonly delicate and refined.

JOHN H. WILLCOX, Mus. Doc.

Adams,	No. 551 Washington Street.
*Albion,	Cor. Beacon and Tremont Sts.
AMERICAN,	No. 56 Hanover Street.
Arlington,	Causeway and Canal Streets.
Boston,	Cor. Beach St. and Harrison Ave.
Centre,	Cor. Washington and Friend Sts.
*Clarendon,	No. 523 Tremont Street.
*Commonwealth,	1697 Washington Street.
*Coolidge,	Bowdoin Square.
Crawford,	Scollay Square.
Creighton,	No. 245 Tremont Street.
Essex.	No. 76½ Essex Street.
*Evans,	No. 175 Tremont Street.
*Everett,	Cor. Wash. and Camden Sts.
*Hotel Bellevue,	No. 17 Beacon Street.
*Hotel Boylston,	Boylston, cor. Tremont Street.
*Hotel Dartmouth,	144 Dudley Street.
*Hotel Dearborn,	Dudley Street.
Hotel Dighton,	Cor. Washington and Dedham Streets.
*Hotel Dudley,	231 Dudley Street.
*Hotel Florence,	Washington, near Florence St.
*Hotel Hamilton,	Cor. Commonwealth Avenue and Clarendon Street.
*Hotel Kempton,	Berkeley, cor. Newbury Street.
*Hotel Madison,	1098 Washington Street.
*Hotel Pelham,	Boylston, cor. Tremont Street, C. Englert.
*Hotel Ruggles,	44 Cambridge, and 4 Hancock Streets, F. E. Ruggles.
*Hotel Somerset,	27 Somerset Street.
*Hotel Tennyson,	Tennyson, cor. Church Street.

WAITERS' JACKETS.

ALWAYS ON HAND,

ALPACA JACKETS and COTTON JACKETS
for Waiters, at

BRINE'S,

365   Washington Street.   365

*Hotel Upton,   14 Upton Street.
*Hotel Vendome,   Commonwealth Avenue, cor.
                         Dartmouth Street, C. A. Wood.
*Hotel Windsor,   103 Shawmut Avenue.
Howard House,   33 Howard Street, Mrs. M. A.
                         Hanson.
Huntington House,   Cortes, near Ferdinand Street.
International,   Hayward Place.
Marlboro',   391 Washington Street.
Maverick,   No. 24 Maverick Square, (E.B.).
Merrimac,   Cor. Merrimac and Friend Sts.
Metropolitan Hotel,   1162 to 1168 Washington Street.
Milliken,   No. 347 Washington Street.
Miller,   Cor. Washington and W. Dover
                         Streets.
National,   Cor. Blackstone and Cross Sts.
New-England,   Cor. Clinton and Blackstone Sts.
*Norfolk,   Eliot Square (R.).
Park,   No. 7 Central Court.
Parker,   No. 60 School Street.
Quincy,   No. 1 Brattle Square.
Revere,   Bowdoin Square.
Selwyn,   No. 29 Harrison Avenue.
Sherman,   Court Square.
*St. Cloud,   Tremont Street, Union Park.
St. Elmo,   No. 27 Boylston Street.
St. James,   Franklin Square.
Temple,   Nos. 8 and 9 Bowdoin Square.
Tremont,   Cor. Tremont and Beacon Sts.
United States,   Cor. Beach and Lincoln Streets.
*Winthrop,   Cor. Bowdoin and Allston Sts.
Young's,   Court Avenue.

Customers can fill their memorandum in every thing in the

SMALL WARE LINE

AT

WM. S. BUTLER & CO.,

90 & 92 Tremont Street.

Brighton.

Cattle Fair Hotel, Charles-river Hotel, Nagle Hotel, Pitman's Hotel, Reservoir House, Riverside House, Rockland House, Seates Hotel.

Restaurants and Cafes.

The stranger in Boston who cannot find a place to satisfy his hunger in any part of the city must be extremely unfortunate. For the guidance of those who do not know where to go, with an assurance that they will be well-served, we insert a list of cafés, restaurants, and confectioners of the best reputation in various parts of Boston; but as the list is short, and does not pretend to be complete, the absence of any saloon or eating-house from it is not to be taken as in any way prejudicial to it. Those where ladies are wont to resort are marked with an asterisk (*).

* *Parker House*, gentlemen's dining-room, ladies' dining-room, and café in the basement, School Street.
* *Revere-House Café*, Bowdoin Square.
* *Copeland's*, No. 4 Tremont Row.
* *Copeland's*, No. 467 Washington Street.
* *Copeland's*, Tremont Street, opposite Park Street.
Young's Hotel, Court Avenue.
Crawford House, Scollay Square.
* *Weber's*, No. 25 Temple Place.
* *Fera's*, No. 525 Washington Street.
Kendall & Dearborn, 8 and 10 Pearl Street.
* *Mrs. Harrington's*, No. 13 School Street.

A. STOWELL & CO.,

16 WINTER STREET,

HAVE FACILITIES FOR REPAIRING ALL KINDS OF

IMPORTED JEWELRY, WHITBY JET, CORAL, CRYSTAL, LAVA,

AND ALL KINDS OF ROMAN GOLD.

* *Dooling's*, Nos. 1447 and 1449 Washington St.
* *Young Women's Christian Association* (ladies only), No. 25 Beach Street.
* *Hotel Boylston Café*, Boylston, near corner of Tremont Street.

Englehardt's, No. 19 Hawley Street.
* *Campbell & Coverly*, No. 233 Washington Street.
* *Isaac Learned & Co.*, No. 413 Washington St.
* *Ober's*, Winter Place.
* *Holly Tree Coffee-House*, 214 Cambridge Street.
* *Wm. Tufts*, under Odd Fellow's Hall, Tremont cor. Berkeley Street.
* *Hotel Belmont*, Nos. 623 and 625 Washington St.
* *Deacon House Café*, Nos. 1635 to 1675 Washington Street.

International, No. 3 Hayward Place.
Smith and Underwood's, 9 Exchange Place.
Fontarive's, 1 Spring Lane.
* *Marston and Cunio's*, 19 School Street.

A. Fellner, 129 Federal.
Boston Young Men's Christian Union, 520 Washington Street.
Tremont House Café, Under Tremont House, Beacon Street side.
Dolliver, Currier, & Co., Milk, cor. Federal.
Edgerly and Crockett, 10 Faneuil Hall Square.
* *Gilman's*, 50 Summer Street.

R. Marston & Co., 23 Brattle Street.
* *Messenger Brothers*, 55 Bromfield Street.
* *R. B. Brigham*, 642 and 644 Washington Street.

Wright's Oyster House, cor. Court and Brattle Sts.

THE

NEW ENGLAND ORGAN CO.

EMPLOY THE

MOST SKILFUL WORKMEN

IN PRODUCING THEIR

UNRIVALLED CABINET ORGANS.

The Seventeenth of June.

Centennial Celebration of the Battle of Bunker Hill.

The following is a condensed statement of the arrangements for the grand celebration of the 17th inst: —

The bells of the churches will be rung for half an hour at sunrise, noon, and sunset.

National Salutes will be fired at the same time at the Navy Yard, Charlestown, and at East Boston, South Boston, Roxbury, West Roxbury, and Brighton.

The East Boston Ferries will run free during the day and evening.

The State House, City Hall, Faneuil Hall, Old South Church, Old North Church, Warren's birth-place, Dorchester Heights, Line of Old Fortifications on the Neck, Old City Hall in Charlestown, and other places of historical interest, will be tastefully decorated. Four thousand flags will be displayed on the Common, and across the streets leading to the Monument grounds. A magnificent arch will be placed at the Charlestown end of Charles River bridge, bearing the names of the principal officers who took part in the battle.

The State House, the dome of the City Hall, and the front and dome of the Old City Hall in Charlestown, will be brilliantly illuminated in the evening by gas jets.

Calcium lights will be exhibited from the following

BLACK FROCKS,
  BLACK PANTALOONS,
    BLACK VESTS.

FULL ASSORTMENT AT

BRINE'S,
365 Washington Street. 365

points: four lights from the top of Bunker Hill Monument; two lights from the top of Dr. Lothrop's church, Back Bay; two from the top of N. J. Bradlee's Observatory at the Highlands; four from the dome of the Commonwealth Hotel (occupied by the State and City's guests); two from a tower on Dorchester Heights, and two from the highest point in East Boston.

There will be a display of rockets, Bengal lights, &c., at four points on the Common, and on Sullivan Square in Charlestown.

Prof. Geo. A. Rogers will make an ascension from the Common at 5 o'clock p. m., in a balloon having a capacity of forty thousand cubic feet.

The procession will be marshalled by Gen. Francis A. Osborn, with Col. W. V. Hutchings as Chief of Staff. The Massachusetts Volunteer Militia, and the military organizations from other States, will form on the Common at about 9 o'clock in the morning, and at 9½ o'clock will move out at the gate opposite Park Sq. (near Providence Depot), and march round the Common past the State House, where they will be reviewed by the Governor, the General Court, the City Council, and the guests of the State and the City. The military part of the procession will then be joined by the civil organizations, the trades, &c., and move over the following route to the Monument grounds. The following is the route of the procession: —

Dartmouth Street will be the basis of formation. From that point the column will move through Columbus Avenue, West Chester Park, Chester Square, southwest side, Washington, and Union Park Streets, Union Park, southwest side, Tremont, Boylston,

---

WM. S. BUTLER & CO.,

IMPORTERS AND RETAILERS OF

MILLINERY GOODS, HOSIERY, GLOVES, SMALL WARES, &c.,

90 TREMONT STREET, BOSTON. 92

NEXT DOOR TO METROPOLITAN R.R. OFFICE.

Washington, Milk, India, Commercial, and South Market Streets, Merchants Row, State, Devonshire, and Washington Streets, Charles River Bridge, Charles River Avenue, City Square, Chelsea, Chestnut, Lexington, Tremont, Concord, Bunker Hill, and Main Streets, Monument Avenue, High and Winthrop Streets, to Winthrop Square, where the procession will be dismissed. The length of the above route is six miles.

On arriving at the Monument Grounds the exercises will be opened with an Anthem by the Apollo Club; to be followed by a Prayer by Rev. Rufus Ellis; a brief introductory address by Hon. G. Washington Warren, President of the Bunker Hill Monument Association; original hymn by the Apollo Club; Oration by Judge Devens; Loyal Song by the Apollo Club; Prayer by Rev. Phillips Brooks; hymn and benediction. The proceedings will take place in a tent capable of seating about six thousand persons.

OTHER CELEBRATIONS.

This is the fifth grand celebration of the Bunker Hill Monument Association. The first occurred in 1825, at the laying of the corner stone of the monument. Daniel Webster delivered his memorable speech, Lafayette was present, and there was a great Masonic display; the second occurred in 1843, on the completion of the monument, oration by Daniel Webster; the third in 1850, on the 75th anniversary of the battle, when Edward Everett delivered an address; the fourth in 1857, at the inauguration of the Warren Statue.

A. STOWELL & CO.,

IMPORTERS OF

FINE WHITBY JET GOODS.

BROOCHES, EARRINGS, SLEEVE BUTTONS, NECKLACES, BRACELETS, PENDANTS, CROSSES, ETC.

The Best Assortment in the Country.

16 WINTER STREET.

www.ingramcontent.com/pod-product-compliance
Lightning Source LLC
Chambersburg PA
CBHW031608110426
42742CB00037B/1335